D0340833

Praise for *Use Your Difference to Make a Difference*

A truly inspiring read and a must for anyone thinking of creating an inclusive culture within their workplace through understanding the role they can play, with detailed explanations of key concepts around Diversity and Inclusion and some powerful ways to create a sense of belonging for all, through understanding key barriers and solutions to inclusion in a globally workable context.

—Asif Sadiq, MBE, Diversity, Inclusion, and Belonging thought leader and global expert

This book is an incredibly thorough piece of thought leadership. Tayo has provided the world with a tool for readers who are interested in diving far beneath the superficial treatment that diversity materials often receive. Anyone intentional enough to read this book will increase their cultural fluency and have access to deeper levels of interpersonal discernment and communication. This book should be required reading in a number of settings.

—Dr. Tiffany Jana, founder of TMI Portfolio and best-selling author of *The B Corp Handbook, Erasing Institutional Bias*, and *Overcoming Bias*

Tayo Rockson meticulously unpacks the complex barriers to leveraging our "difference to make a difference" and provides tangible solutions to counter those forces while we hold fast to our core values.

—Tsedal Neeley, Harvard Business School professor and author of *The Language of Global Success*

Tayo beautifully acknowledges our differences as superpowers, and how our unique positionalities can be used as tools to bridge across divides. He interweaves his global upbringing in a proactive and interactive manner throughout the book; it feels as though you're having a one-on-one dialogue with him.

—Liz Kleinrock, founder of Teach and Transform

This is a great primer for us all to reflect on our own part in the current divisiveness in our workplaces and world places with fantastic ideas on ways to move forward to connect and create—together. It's a book to share with everyone on your team to create an environment of less ego, more openness, and more possibilities!

—Cy Wakeman, *New York Times* best-selling author, drama researcher, and author of *No Ego*

This book is a must-read for all Diversity and Inclusion professionals; it's a wonderfully constructed manual that will ensure inclusive corporate environments.

—Caroline Codsi, ICD.D., president and founder, Women in Governance

Tayo Rockson is an authentic voice for our times. He possesses the rare ability to draw on his own personal story, combine it with his highly developed intellect and commitment to knowledge, and deliver a truly tangible set of learning steps and action items for us all. Along with an unquenchable thirst for cultural learning and understanding, he displays a deep passion for serving our global human family. This is a not only a contemporary book for our current times but is one whose message will have a profound impact on generations to come.

—Brett D. Parry, founder and CEO, Cultural Mentor

Tayo Rockson's deep passion for "using his difference to make a difference" comes through loud and clear in his handy new book, which is chock-full of information and ideas to improve your cultural competence skills.

—Andy Molinsky, Brandeis professor and author of *Global Dexterity* & *Reach*

Tayo Rockson

USE YOUR

Difference

TO MAKE A

Difference

HOW TO CONNECT AND COMMUNICATE
IN A CROSS-CULTURAL WORLD

WILEY

Copyright © 2019 by John Wiley & Sons, Inc. All rights reserved.

Published by John Wiley & Sons, Inc., Hoboken, New Jersey.
Published simultaneously in Canada.

No part of this publication may be reproduced, stored in a retrieval system, or transmitted in any form or by any means, electronic, mechanical, photocopying, recording, scanning, or otherwise, except as permitted under Section 107 or 108 of the 1976 United States Copyright Act, without either the prior written permission of the Publisher, or authorization through payment of the appropriate per-copy fee to the Copyright Clearance Center, Inc., 222 Rosewood Drive, Danvers, MA 01923, (978) 750-8400, fax (978) 646-8600, or on the Web at www.copyright.com. Requests to the Publisher for permission should be addressed to the Permissions Department, John Wiley & Sons, Inc., 111 River Street, Hoboken, NJ 07030, (201) 748-6011, fax (201) 748-6008, or online at http://www.wiley.com/go/permissions.

Limit of Liability/Disclaimer of Warranty: While the publisher and author have used their best efforts in preparing this book, they make no representations or warranties with respect to the accuracy or completeness of the contents of this book and specifically disclaim any implied warranties of merchantability or fitness for a particular purpose. No warranty may be created or extended by sales representatives or written sales materials. The advice and strategies contained herein may not be suitable for your situation. You should consult with a professional where appropriate. Neither the publisher nor author shall be liable for any loss of profit or any other commercial damages, including but not limited to special, incidental, consequential, or other damages.

For general information on our other products and services or for technical support, please contact our Customer Care Department within the United States at (800) 762-2974, outside the United States at (317) 572-3993 or fax (317) 572-4002.

Wiley publishes in a variety of print and electronic formats and by print-on-demand. Some material included with standard print versions of this book may not be included in e-books or in print-on-demand. If this book refers to media such as a CD or DVD that is not included in the version you purchased, you may download this material at http://booksupport.wiley.com. For more information about Wiley products, visit www.wiley.com.

Library of Congress Cataloging-in-Publication Data

Names: Rockson, Tayo, author.
Title: Use your difference to make a difference : how to connect and
    communicate in a cross-cultural world / Tayo Rockson.
Description: Hoboken, New Jersey : John Wiley & Sons, Inc., [2019] | Includes
    index. |
Identifiers: LCCN 2019017165 (print) | LCCN 2019019089 (ebook) | ISBN
    9781119590729 (Adobe PDF) | ISBN 9781119590736 (ePub) | ISBN 9781119590699
    (hardcover)
Subjects: LCSH: Intercultural communication. | Interpersonal relations. |
    Toleration. | Multiculturalism.
Classification: LCC HM1211 (ebook) | LCC HM1211 .R635 2019 (print) | DDC
    305.8—dc23
LC record available at https://lccn.loc.gov/2019017165

COVER DESIGN: PAUL McCARTHY
COVER BACKGROUND ART: © GETTY IMAGES / R.TSUBIN

Printed in the United States of America

V10012384 072619

This book is dedicated to all those who have been told that they were too weird, too strange, too big, too little, or invisible. I want you to know that you matter. Your quirks are your superpowers. I see you. I hear you. I affirm you and I love you!

Contents

Foreword

A s a global educator, I have had the opportunity to teach children of diplomats, personal growth icons, teachers, secretaries, CEOs, actresses, film directors, and some of the most amazing minds I could ever imagine. People often ask me, "What do these parents teach their children about success?" I completely understand the intention behind the question. People want to know if there are any secrets or tips that they could also gift their children. But what's interesting is that oftentimes when people reach a certain level of affluence, they realize that there are actually three types of success: success in health, success in wealth, and success in relationships. The third is measured by impact. Therefore, what is discussed in these spaces is that parents truly want their children to understand that being a millionaire also means impacting a million lives. What's beautiful about having an impact is that you can do it right now. And do you know how to determine whether or not you have given someone an impactful experience?

You know when someone has experienced impact when they refer to how their thoughts or actions have changed rather than simply praising the person they have learned from. People who experience impact say things like, "Oh my goodness, after I had a conversation with Person A, I started to think about my relationship with my own family and decided to do things differently." People who may not have been impacted, but may have been inspired, say things like, "Wow! Person A is amazing." If you truly want to leave your mark on the world, go for impact.

My initial connection to Tayo was by way of his impact. All across social media, individuals identified how they'd felt seen and acknowledged when listening to Tayo's podcast, *As Told By Nomads*, witnessing one of his many TEDx talks, or consuming his posts online. They discussed what they were doing differently and ways his words shifted their perspectives. People connected with his work and publicly remarked upon its power.

After having redesigned learning programs in more than 20 countries, I knew that this wasn't simply greatness that I wanted to have proximity to. I wanted to share it with my students! I wanted them to know Tayo and directly experience his unique form of impact-bringing light to the importance of diversity and inclusion. Tayo's message, "use your difference to make a difference," introduced inclusion as a lifestyle that my students could wear as badges of honor as they stepped out into the world with pride and certainty. Tayo has always been very eager to share his perspectives with my students and over the course of two years I have connected Tayo with students from over 40 countries.

As a facilitator and guide, it has been beautiful to witness the healing that has taken place. After engaging in one conversation with Tayo, my South Korean student, Daniel, who'd stopped "trying" in school after a teacher referred to him as "average," felt empowered to decide his own life philosophy and adopted the belief that his opinions mattered. He went from being the kid who rarely completed homework assignments to joining the debate team, winning national speaking competitions, and getting straight A's. Introducing young people to the importance of diversity and inclusion also teaches them the importance of their individuality and gives them permission to embrace their own uniqueness. This topic heals all of those involved.

There's a popular saying that was shared among my peers in education in South Korea, "I become more of who I want to be every time I read a book." As an educator, I want that for you. Inclusion is acknowledgment; it's connection. It's an "I see you." It's "You can sit with us." It's . . . "I believe in you." True inclusion not only heals, but it empowers both those who witness and those who experience.

As a global educator, I challenge you to not only read this book, but to slather on the learnings like lotion and wear them daily. Read each section of the book and ask yourself, "How will I live this today?" Live your learning. A good book will show you, but an impactful book will grow you. In this moment, no matter how old you are or where you are in your journey of lifelong learning, I am stepping in for your teacher and saying, I'm so proud of you for taking such a powerful step toward your growth. I see you. You can sit with me. I believe in you.

—Gahmya Drummond-Bey, global educator,
curriculum designer, and TED speaker

Acknowledgments

In many ways, writing this book has been a dream come true and a source of tremendous joy for me. When I started writing poems back in 10th grade, I couldn't envision doing this, so I am incredibly humbled and grateful for the opportunity to share this book with you. It is a culmination of all my personal and professional observations as someone who has lived in the intersections. None of this would have been possible without God, my lord and savior; I can't even count the ways I have felt Her presence. To my parents, Akinkunmi and Iyabosola Rockson, thank you for providing a stable home to always come back to, despite the ups and downs. I could always count on you two to send me inspirational videos, pictures, and/or articles to keep me going throughout the week. The perseverance, discipline, perspective, tough love, manners, respect, and so much more that you taught me have helped me succeed in life.

I'm also eternally grateful to my brothers, Dele and Tunde Rockson. Both of you challenged me to be a better leader, brother, and man. You both make me so proud with how much you do.

To Rob Kingyens, who took a chance on a freshly graduated young man in Virginia and again when I moved to New York City. You saw someone raw who you could mentor. Thank you for that!

To Sasha Reed, who was the first person to invest in me. I am still so humbled by how much of a chance you took on me. Thank you for seeing me even when I could not see myself.

To Charlotte Maiorana, for introducing me to John Wiley & Sons and to Karen Jaw-Madson, for your constant follow-up emails to make sure I got the attention of your publisher.

The time I spent writing this book would not have been complete without my amazing support system of friends. Gahmya Drummond-Bey, Kris Alanna Wilson A.K.A Purple, Zahra Ghazal Sakhi, Rachel Padmini Kumar, Amanda Joy, Liz Kleinrock, Daniella Veras, and Jenn Halweil. A very special thanks to you eight for the late nights, the encouragement, and the constant reminder of my ability to complete this book. We have been through so many things together. Thank you so much!

I'm forever indebted to both the late Nelson Mandela and Oprah Winfrey for inspiring me to embark on this journey as a speaker, writer, consultant, and media personality. I always wished I could meet you, Madiba, but I know I will soon enough. You taught me how to look at the bigger picture of life and to seek compassion. Oprah, you encouraged me to live my best life and, because of your platforms, I always found a home when I was lost. To Vicki Adang, for your editorial help and breathing life into my stories and anecdotes. To Jeanenne Ray, for taking a chance on me and helping me become part of the Wiley family.

Finally, the warmest of hugs to all those who have been a part of my getting here: Sandra Revueltas, Daniela Tudor, Roxana Colorado, Mimi Zheng, Lina Abisoghomyan, Mina Salib, Daniella Veras, and Austin Belcak.

Introduction

The first time I vividly remember thinking about the impact of connection was May 29, 1999. As a Nigerian, I was seated on my family couch in Eric Moore Towers, Surulere, Lagos, deeply captivated by the television screen. I imagine millions of other Nigerians were as well. We were about to transition into civilian rule for the first time since I was born.

That's right. I was born into a dictatorship and the regimes I witnessed were oppressive, to say the least. One of my earliest memories was when I was three years old. I heard many cries and groans of disappointment from people outside my family's compound because our recently held democratic election results had been annulled. Moshood Abiola, the man who was democratically elected by most Nigerians at the time, was denied victory; the uproar it sparked was so great that it led to another coup. We watched as another dictator took his throne on Aso Rock, which, for those wondering, is our equivalent of the White House.

Everything I had witnessed up until May 29, 1999 was what many would classify as classic authoritarianism: muzzling of the press, suppression of opponents, and countless human rights violations. In addition, many of Nigeria's 250-plus ethnic groups were vying for ethnic domination because they had been ingeniously excluded from positions of national leadership. Let's call this the gift of **colonialism** (more about colonialism is in the glossary).

All this led me to wonder what it was like to be seen, heard, and understood for who I really was.

So as I sat there in the living room watching as General Abdul-salami Abubakar handed over power to Olusegun Obasanjo (a former military ruler himself), I wondered what type of leader it would take to bring a bunch of people who held different values and saw the world differently together.

I wondered how he would get people to connect.

Little did I know that my adventure was about to start: about a year after that inauguration, my dad's job as a diplomat began to take us all over the world.

My first stop was Ouagadougou, Burkina Faso. Here, I found myself as this skinny Nigerian kid with a thick Nigerian accent in a French-speaking country in an American school going through … puberty!

Yup!

Even in a place where everybody felt different, I felt different.

I sometimes felt like a fish out of water in Nigeria, but multiply that feeling by a hundred and you might understand what it felt like for me to search for my voice in my new environment.

I mean, this was the first time I remember seeing white people outside of my television screen.

I had previously lived in Sweden during the dictatorship years, but I was a baby, so I don't remember anything from that experience. So, yes, for all intents and purposes, this was my first time seeing people with different skin tones outside of my television screen.

I looked around for ways to connect.

My default for doing that had always been sports, and back then, the only sport I played was soccer. However, I saw that most people played basketball, so I did what any 10- or 11-year-old would do when he/she wants to learn a new sport.

I went to the library!

Yup, I checked out all the books I could find on basketball. I found out that there were two doctors in basketball: Dr. Naismith, who invented basketball, and Dr. J, who played for the Sixers. I checked out the latest *Sports Illustrated for Kids* magazines to familiarize myself with the current basketball players.

Once I felt like I knew everything there was to know about the sport, I decided I needed to know how to apply what I had learned, so I went to the best basketball player I knew, Michael Albright, and asked him nervously if he could help. I was like, "Uhh, Michael. I know everything about the game, *but* can you teach me how to actually play it?" Thankfully, he said yes, and our 1-on-1s became 2-on-2s, then 3-on-3s, then 4-on-4s, and then 5-on-5s.

All of a sudden, it didn't matter where we all came from. I had a Taiwanese teammate, an American teammate, an Ivorian teammate, a Dutch teammate, and a Cameroonian teammate, and we had a common goal—which was to win.

A common goal. That was my first clue.

Establishing mutual purpose is key when you want to connect across cultures, which we'll talk about later, *but* on that court, what we were learning to do was how to leverage our differences to work together.

That one experience opened my eyes to the possibility of what a world could look like if we connected across differences. It also led me down this quest of exploring different environments to find the best ways to forge these connections and build bridges.

I did all this not only because of my background as someone who was now going to be a minority everywhere he went, but also because I firmly believe that learning how to connect across cultures is how all of us can change the world.

If we look around us today, we can see that, thanks to the Internet, migration patterns and new markets keep popping up and we are experiencing a whole new world. The intersections of markets, customers, ideas, religions, and world views are shifting and influencing our priorities today and will continue to influence them tomorrow.

Essentially, leaders of today and tomorrow must know how to succeed with all these differences. The world is changing, and instead of resisting that reality, we must seek to understand it so that we can leverage our differences the right way.

There isn't a country that is solely comprised of natives anymore. Due to mass migration, millions of people move for various reasons: they move for better opportunities, education, jobs, and much more. Another thing you'll notice is that the Internet has created a system where at any given time, people are able to connect across the globe. Due to this globalization, individuals and businesses need to build their cultural competency levels in order to understand and leverage their differences. The world is much more complex than it has ever been and with that comes inevitable interactions among all sorts of cultures. The fact of the matter is that globalization is here and not going away. Yet a lot of the world hasn't caught up. Global leadership is more important than it has ever been before. In short, we live in a diverse world. You cannot lead, motivate, and inspire the people around you if you're not able to create inclusive environments that allow each of them to feel comfortable enough to be themselves.

The journey I have taken for the past 18 years has led me to the answer to a question that I have been curious about for most of my life, which is, how does one connect effectively across cultures?

The type of people who know how to connect effectively do three things:

1. They **Educate**.
2. They **Don't Perpetuate**.
3. **Instead,** they **Communicate**.

These three things are the bedrocks of connection and they make up what I call the Connection IQ, or CIQ. My goal is to show people how to raise their level of awareness and consciousness so they can connect to themselves as well as cross-culturally and how to do these three things the right way so people can take advantage of the globalization and the digitalization that are going on around us.

But first, let's dive into why I wrote this book.

Why I Wrote This Book

Throughout history, it has been the inaction of those who could have acted; the indifference of those who should have known better; the silence of the voice of justice when it mattered most; that has made it possible for evil to triumph.

—Haile Selassie

I wrote this book because we are in a time of deep divisions and I believe that now, more than ever, we need to learn how to cultivate. Today's culture is defined by fear, uncertainty, intolerance, and reactiveness. It feels like a war zone sometimes because in a world of nuance, we are governed by binary systems.

In addition to this, we are losing faith in many of our foundational institutions (religion, education, government, family, the Internet, the media).

This isn't happening in just some places; it's happening all over the world.

There simply isn't any clarity on what we find threatening, because we all feel things differently.

Despite this, I'm filled with hope, because we are also in the midst of an awakening of sorts—an awakening that allows us to see who we are really are and where we can improve.

The world has to awaken every now and then to the fact that we are responsible for the world we get.

My objective with this book is to bring together people who hold different beliefs so they can get to know each other and create a path toward moral courage, empathy, compassion, and accountability. There are times when you have to stop being a bystander, and I hope that this book provides you with practical skill sets that you can use to transcend barriers and define values to advance humanity.

We are bonded by our need to connect and advance, so let's connect and advance toward a more inclusive world.

My mission statement is: Use your *difference* to make a *difference*. It is the credo I live by and is what this book is based on. It is about celebrating the fullness and breadth of ourselves. It is about opening our minds to people so that we can bridge divides and forge connections. I want to bring East and West together and have them sit side by side with North and South to trade stories of adventures and experiences they each have had. I strive to share experiences as a way to connect people of all cultures, to turn discrimination into appreciation, encourage diversity, tell stories to build global mindsets, and to educate the world about the beauty in all of us and how we can work together to embrace our global identities.

Voice

For a lot of my life, I wondered what to do with
my voice.
It never seemed like I had a choice.
I look like this so I must sound like that.
I come from there so I must be like this.

Don't be too loud, they said, you'll scare them.
Don't be too soft, they said, you'll embarrass us.
All these rules, and yet, no space for expression
of self.
Nuance taken away in the name of systems and
expectations.
Identity stripped away to make people I barely
know comfortable.

I rehearsed several versions of myself so I could
play in whatever movie was showing for the
day.
All this hard work, only to play supporting
characters or extras.

I was never the star because God forbid I be
seen as too extra.
So I did what they said.
I became an actor in my own life instead of
THE director.

That was before I heard the power in the sound
of my voice.
What a day it was because I could finally use it
to rejoice.
My voice led me to the hidden layers I had
covered up.
I could finally see myself without any apologies.
My voice led me to the mic so I could project
even more.
Yes! No more hiding.
My voice taught me a lot! But, more
importantly, it brought me to this realization.

Your approval will not make or break me.
Your DISapproval will no longer silence me.
I'm not placed here to make you feel
comfortable about your choices.

My existence isn't something you can tokenize
and my story isn't something you will
weaponize.

I've decided to quit playing your game and the
only game I'll play now is to live up to my
name.

A warrior who brings joy!
Not someone that plays coy.

—Tayo Rockson

What Is Connection?

Noun: **Connection**[1]

1. The act of connecting: the state of being connected
2. Something that connects
3. A person connected with another, especially by marriage, kinship, or common interest has powerful connections
4. A political, social, professional, or commercial relationship
5. A set of persons associated together

Basic principles. Everyone wants to connect in some way, shape, or form.

We want to connect to something, someone, or somewhere. Connecting creates a sense of belonging and it is at the base of our humanity as social animals. We are primed to connect.

Connection is also at the base of every issue we have today when we don't get it right.

Don't believe me?

Take a look at how our inability to connect has affected us throughout history:

◆ **Colonialism:** Telling people that, based on their language, tribe, or religion, they were unable to connect.
◆ **Slavery:** Telling people that they were subhuman so they couldn't possibly connect.

- ◆ **Segregation:** Telling people that they couldn't connect because they looked different.
- ◆ **Apartheid:** A world where you, your spouse, and your kid cannot connect because of the color of your skin.
- ◆ **Crusades:** A series of religious wars fought because of an unwillingness to connect with foreign religions.
- ◆ **Genocide:** The urge to wipe out a part of an ethnic, racial, religious, or national group because of a refusal to connect.
- ◆ **Nationalism I mean Populism I mean Isolationism:** A refusal to connect with other nations except on your own terms.
- ◆ **Racism:** A refusal to connect with someone who has a different skin color.

I could go on and on, but the consistent theme that you can see here is the blaming of the "other" because of a disconnect, either real or perceived.

Crimes of humanity have been committed and rationalized in the name of disconnection.

We have been here before and we are still here now.

The only difference is that the disconnection that was once covert is now overt and the disconnection that was overt is now covert.

Let that sink in ...

It's happening all over the world through globalization, the Internet, and in places without Internet.

We have to push through, though, because as physician and researcher Dr. Dean Ornish once said,

> The need for connection and community is primal, as fundamental as the need for air, water, and food.

It is as fundamental as the need for air, water, and food, so let's honor this need. I wrote the following poem while thinking about my life growing up and the world today.

Walls vs. Bridges

I reached out to connect.
But I was met with no interest.
My bridge came crashing into your wall.

I wondered what caused this stall.
Will it ever fall?
So I sat and observed
as you continued to layer your walls
with bricks of sameness, fear, hate, and a false
sense of security.
This is how you found your happy.
To you, I've never been an option.
I seem to be as dark and unknown as what's
hidden in the depths of the ocean.
Instead of getting to know me,
you've weaponized your friends and family
to be afraid of me.
These stories you tell of me
They are exaggerated and limited.
These walls you built to protect yourself
from me.
They are enclosed spaces with the same ole
faces.
Here's what you've missed while living in
your bubble.
Your barriers have become outliers.
Your limited scope has inspired hope.
I will not just be tolerated. I will be appreciated
As your walls continue to crack, and you
continue to attack,
My revolution will be televised and I will no
longer be generalized.
I reached out to connect.
But I was met with no interest.
My bridge came crashing into your wall and
caused it to fall.
I looked behind me and I saw I wasn't alone.
Together, we built a bridge and knocked down
the walls.

—Tayo Rockson

Here's to building bridges and not walls. Allons y!

How to Use This Book

The book is broken down into three sections. Each section represents what I believe to be the three stages of connection.

The "Educate" section is the foundational piece of the framework, and is needed if you want to master connection to yourself and your environment.

The "Don't Perpetuate" section is focused on helping you know how to navigate the systemic barriers to connection.

The "Instead, Communicate" section is aimed at giving you the tools to connect with people who have different values from you.

Sprinkled throughout the book are poems I have written that reflect the themes I am covering.

At the end of each section, I'll walk you through the application of each stage by using what I call the LORA model. LORA is the acronym that stands for Listen, Observe, Reflect, and Act. These skill sets are the best ways to maximize your potential as you go through each section and will include questions and exercises that will help you improve your listening, observation, reflecting, and acting skills.

Enjoy, and take notes!

Note

1. "Connection." Merriam-Webster, https://www.merriam-webster.com/dictionary/connection.

Part I

Educate

1

Education

Education is the most powerful weapon which you can use to change the world.

—Nelson Mandela

To me, true education involves a few things—IQ, EQ, and CQ, or intelligence quotient, emotional intelligence, and cultural intelligence—that allow us to get a better sense of who we truly are, how others see us, how we fit into the world around us, and the implications of our actions. Essentially, what we are after here is the education of ourselves and education of our environments.

If we don't know who we are, we won't be able to know what to work on in order to become better connectors, so let's get into what makes up your internal culture. Education of self has to do with understanding your internal culture and education of environment has to do with understanding your external culture.

Both of these cultures involve listening and observing. Gaining mastery of your internal cultures is about listening and observing your biases as well as your core values, and gaining mastery of your external cultures is about listening and observing what is around you.

2

Education of Self (Internal Culture)

What Does Your Bias Say about You?

The first thing to understand about your internal culture is your bias. Bias is an inclination or prejudice for or against one person or group. Unconscious bias is the unconscious feelings we have toward other people and groups. Being biased doesn't automatically make us racist or sexist. Biases are human inclinations and ways for us to make decisions in life. Biases allow us to make shortcuts as we go about our days and act as a filter. They are the ways we categorize, view, perceive, remember, connect, and learn about culture.

Although this emotion is not always negative, examining your own possible biases is an important step to understanding the roots of stereotypes and prejudices in our society today. These biases inform *every* decision we make (what we teach, who we hire, who we fire, who we promote, the marketing programs and policies we create and/or support).

Understanding Unconscious Bias

As a diversity and inclusion consultant, I lead a lot of unconscious bias workshops. One of the things I do is to list out the most common types of biases that influence our everyday lives. I go through them because it is important for me to show my clients how their inherent biases translate ambiguous pieces of information into meaningful thoughts. I want people to see how our biases impact connection in the following ways:

- ◆ Our worldviews: how we see people and the world.
- ◆ Our attitudes and behaviors: how we react toward certain people or groups of people based on our worldviews.
- ◆ Our attention: what we pay attention and listen to, consciously or unconsciously.
- ◆ Our comfort level: how safe or unsafe we feel in certain situations.

As you can imagine, all these will affect your drive and desire to connect, so it is important to paint the picture of what is going on in your mind before you make decisions.

That being said, the following are the most common unconscious biases that influence our world today.

Affinity bias: Affinity bias occurs when we see someone we feel we have an affinity with (e.g., we support the same teams, we attended the same college, we come from the same place, or they remind us of someone we know and like). For example, I am obsessed with Harry Potter, Lebron James, and Manchester United, so if I come across anyone who shares an affinity for those things, the chances of me wanting to connect with that person are probably high.

Attribution bias: Attribution refers to how we explain behavior or the cause and effect of something. It's attaching meaning to something, so attribution bias would be attributing someone's behavior to their intrinsic nature. For example, say you're driving and someone cuts you off. You notice that the person has a New Jersey license plate, so you immediately assume that the driver is is careless because he's from Jersey. Now anytime you see a driver from Jersey, your bias is activated. What is missing in this scenario is the failure to assess the situational factors that led to your getting cut off. Instead, a leap was made to attach a meaning to the intrinsic nature of someone.

Beauty bias: This refers to how we judge people based on their physical appearance, especially when they are considered attractive. Unconsciously, many of us associate appearance with personality, so, for example, a tall person might translate as a good leader to you or a beautiful person might be perceived as more trustworthy.

Confirmation bias: This refers to the tendency to gather and process information by looking for, or interpreting, information that is consistent with your existing beliefs. An example of this would be if you were a hiring manager and you think people from certain ethnic groups make for bad employees, so you start looking for evidence that only supports this belief to justify your decision not to hire people from that group.

Conformity bias: This refers to a tendency to behave like those around you rather than using your own personal judgment, even if it's against your personal interest. Maybe everyone around you has decided to go to a certain school and you elect to go along with their decision, even though the school doesn't have what you want to study.

Contrast effect or contrast bias: This refers to the tendency to enhance or diminish something in a large grouping after a single comparison with one of its peers; it doesn't factor in the whole group. I see this often when human resource administrative groups are going through applications for students or prospective employees. For instance, you could be going through a bunch of resumes and applications with identical grade point averages (GPAs) and when you notice an application or resume that has a higher or lower GPA, you decide to admit or deny the student based on the contrast. This is a bias because of the assumption that the GPA is indicative of skill set; often, people who have this bias do not look at other aspects of the resume to see how the applicant could be a great fit for the school or company.

Gender bias: Gender bias is a preference or prejudice toward one gender over the other. This one is pretty self-explanatory.

Halo effect: This refers to one characteristic of a person causing you to view that person positively. Maybe someone has done a TED talk in the past and you immediately overlook all other information about the person because in your mind this person is to be respected. This is similar to affinity and confirmation bias.

Horns effect: This is the direct opposite of the halo effect and it occurs when a characteristic about a person negatively impacts how you view him or her. Maybe you hear that someone you meet is a felon and your mind immediately goes to "hmm, this person must be a bad person."

Negativity bias: This refers to focusing on the negative aspects of what is happening around us. Research by several neuroscientists, including psychologist Dr. Rick Hansen, suggests that the amygdala part of our brain uses about two-thirds of its neurons to look for bad news.[1]

Positivity bias: This refers to people evaluating an individual positively even when they have negative evaluations of the group to which that individual belongs. It is commonly seen within political science literature that examines positive respondent evaluations of individual political leaders in spite of that respondent's negative views on government in general.[2]

Microaggressions: Microaggression is a term that has been used in academic circles since the 1970s to describe small casual verbal and behavioral indignities against people of color, women, people with disabilities, immigrants, young or old people, and so forth. They are regular verbal, nonverbal, and environmental slights, snubs, or insults that can be intentional or unintentional. They come across as hostile, and derogatory and are usually based on your group membership. Repeated over time, they can sometimes lead to stress and high blood pressure.

Examples of microaggressions are as follows:

- "I never see you as a black woman/man/person."
- Telling a person of color that he/she/they sound white or articulate.
- Asking someone you view as racially ambiguous and saying something like "So, like what are you?" and then proceeding to argue with them if you are not satisfied with the answer.

- Approaching someone from any racial group or sexual orientation and saying that they are pretty for a [racial group/sexual orientation] person.
- Calling every Asian you know Chinese because you see Asians as a monolith.
- Calling everyone from Latin American Mexican because you see Latin Americans as a monolith.

As you can see, biases can be either conscious and unconscious. They are formed as a result of programming and the socialization of the culture around us. Our brain automatically categorizes, evaluates, and compares things based on the information it receives. So this begs the question, How can we objectively monitor our programming?

The answer?

By reflecting on our experiences.

To better understand your experiences, ask yourself the following questions. I call this the power of three.

The Power of Three

Who are your three best friends?
What are their ethnic backgrounds?

What do they believe in?

What do you bond over or argue about?

What are their orientations, religion, genders, and so on?

What other information can you think of?

Where are the last three places you've lived in?
What are the characteristics of those places? Suburban, rural, metropolitan?

Describe the socioeconomic makeup of those places.

(Continued)

> *Who are the last three people you've been in relationships with?*
>
> What are their ethnic backgrounds?
>
> What do they believe in?
>
> What do you bond over or argue about?
>
> What are their orientations, religion, genders, and so on?
>
> What other information you can think of?

Take your time and be as thorough as you can. I ask these questions to show you where your opinions and your preferences might have come from. My hope is that you're able to see how some of the decisions you make today are based on your experiences. I also wanted to give you insight into who makes up your sphere of influence. Your **sphere of influence** is anyone in your circle who has the power to influence you or you have the ability to influence—your friends, family, significant others, teachers, or mentors.

Identifying Prejudices

After this, let's go into the "How biased am I?" section, which looks at the stereotypes, prejudices, and biases you believe you hold right now. Typically we hold prejudices for four reasons—story, fear, security, or avoidance.

1. **Story**—based on the religion, education, or philosophy that has been passed on from your sphere of influence.
2. **Fear**—based on a bad experience you or someone in your sphere of influence experienced.
3. **Security**—a way for you to feel safe and better about yourself.
4. **Avoidance**—a way to dodge difficult situations with groups you don't understand or groups that make you feel uncomfortable.

Name the stereotypes you believe (positive and negative) and list out the reasons you feel like you have them. There's no shame in revealing all these. As stated before, this is what makes us human. Just be honest with yourself. If you're having problems identifying your biases, I encourage you to take the Implicit Association Test from Harvard at https://implicit.harvard.edu/implicit/.[3]

The main habit I want you to develop here is to learn how to repeatedly question your assumptions. Constantly ask yourself if you would come to the same conclusion you initially did about different people after you examine your biases. If so, ask yourself why. Also, consistently put yourself out there and hold yourself accountable.

Knowing Your Emotional Triggers

As you discover the reasons you have your biases, you will come across your emotional triggers. Emotional triggers are situations, people, images, words, sounds, opinions, or environmental situations that evoke emotional reactions within us. They typically happen as a result of a trauma, fear, or someone opposing your values.

Personally, I occasionally get triggered when I hear loud sharp noises because it reminds me of the near-death experience I faced on August 22, 2012. I was in a three-car accident in which my car was completely totaled. Now, whenever I'm in a car that suddenly accelerates too quickly or if I hear a loud noise, I'm briefly transported to that day and I briefly experience chills or nausea. It also happens sometimes when I see a car accident in a movie or on TV. The same thing could happen to you if:

You find yourself experiencing a trauma again.

Your ego feels threatened.

Your beliefs are challenged.

If you fail to recognize your triggers, your emotions can become unchecked—and left unchecked, they can become anger, fear, hatred, sadness, anxiety, and much more. These emotions are all barriers to connection to yourself and others. Another consequence of not checking in with your emotions is that you will end up being controlled by them. This keeps your bias in charge.

We don't want that, so in order to get ahead of this, I encourage you to start a **Bias Journal** or a diary of your biases and emotional triggers. This journal will be used to focus your attention on your biases and triggers as well as to record your progress or lack thereof.

Keeping a Bias Journal

Create two sections in your journal, one titled Emotional Triggers and the other titled Biases.

In the Emotional Triggers section, record the following:

◆ How does your body react when your emotions go off? What is it telling you and what is it reacting to?
◆ Who or what triggered the emotion?
◆ What needs of yours weren't being met at that moment?

Documenting this will allow you to understand your tendencies, body language, and tone when you're mad, happy, nervous, and so on.

In the Bias section, do the same thing:

◆ Write out any generalizations that you notice yourself making.
◆ Document how many times you put yourself in a position where you're the minority in a group.
◆ Document why you make the decisions you do or come to the conclusions you do on a daily basis.

Also be on the lookout for when your biases flare up the most. Typically, they flare up:

◆ When we are under stress.
◆ When we are under time constraints.

(Continued)

◆ When we are multitasking.
◆ When there's a lack of information.
◆ When we are tired.

Please take your bias journal very seriously, because the best way to deautomatize your biases is to first acknowledge them, then put yourself in a position where you actually experience the discomfort of understanding what you don't understand. All these questions allow you to challenge your biases, correct them, and get used to equally good alternatives.

We can't overcome any of our biases or triggers if we are not aware of them.

Notice I said equally good alternatives; the idea here is to show you that your way isn't the only way.

Understanding your internal culture gives you insight not only into who you are and how your behavior affects others, it also gives you insight into the in-groups and out-groups that exist around you—basically, who you unintentionally exclude in social settings.

Generally we create relationships with people who are most like us, and there's nothing necessarily wrong with this. But if we *only* do this, we can end up creating a reinforcing cycle because our comfort zone gets fortified and once it's fortified, our experiences remain largely the same. If our experiences remain largely the same, stereotypes are formed.

So *change your experiences*!

The Goal Here Is to Learn, Unlearn, and Relearn

As you have seen, our environments shape us consciously and subconsciously, and in order for us to be more in control of our programming, we need to pursue experiences. In today's fast-paced world, we don't get to reflect on who are and who we are becoming. Instead, we react to what we think we know.

As you go through these exercises, you will find yourself either reevaluating or questioning your core values.

It just so happens that understanding your core values is the last aspect of self-education.

Notes

1. Margaret Jaworski, "The Negativity Bias: Why the Bad Stuff Sticks and How to Overcome It," *PsyCom.net*, 8 June 2018, www.psycom.net/ negativity-bias.
2. "Positivity Bias," in P. Lavrakas, *Encyclopedia of Survey Research Methods* (Sage, 2008), methods.sagepub.com/reference/encyclopedia-of-survey-research-methods/n387.xml.
3. Project Implicit, *Select a Test*, https://implicit.harvard.edu/implicit/.

3

What Are Your Core Values?

Y our core values are your fundamental beliefs as a person. They also can guide your decision making. In Chapter 2, we went over how biases can play a role into the choices you make. Now, I want you to be intentional and use your core values, instead of your biases, to make decisions. You will develop your own personal code of conduct, which will allow you to become your most authentic self. Think of Superman. No matter what setting he's in, he is guided by Truth, Justice, and what he believes to be the American Way. Here's an alien who, orphaned, found himself brought in by an unsuspecting couple in Kansas. As he grew older and learned about himself and the world, he realized he had superpowers that his earthly neighbors weren't gifted with. But instead of deciding to be a dictator, he decided to use his power for good.

Why?

He certainly didn't have to do good. In fact, one could argue that it's a burden to do be Earth's savior—but he chose to fight for humanity anyway.

He did this because of his core values and what he believed to be right, and this has seen him saving good and morally bankrupt people alike. He lived in accordance with his core values. My question for you all today is this: Do you live in accordance with your core values or outside them?

We are currently at an inflection point in the world today where we need to decide who we are and who we want to be. The gap between who we are and who we want to be is what our lives are all about. The way we get to become the person we want to become is through understanding our personal core values. Core values inform our drive, motivations, and what is important to us; without drive or motivation, there is no action. And no action means no actual connection. Much like your biases, your values can operate on autopilot. Your core values are essentially your heart and soul. Think of your core values as your compass: they are the essence of your character.

I find that core values don't matter unless you're living them and if you're living them, they should be consistent with the person you want to become. Carl Jung once said, "You are what you do, not what you say you'll do," and he couldn't be more right. A lot of the disconnect we see today is because people aren't consistently living out their values.

I believe a lot of people in the world currently live outside of their core values because we have let the fear of being rejected, ostracized, or singled out overtake our desire to do what we feel is right. What happens in the process is that our curiosity has gotten stifled, and when our curiosity gets stifles, our brains only act on what makes them feel comfortable, which ultimately becomes habit for us.

Now that we know why core values matter, let's go over how you can articulate them.

Articulating Your Core Values

In order to understand your core values, you need to do a deep dive into the pivotal moments in your life and your favorite characters. List all the significant moments in your life up to this point and for each moment, describe what was happening, what values you were honoring then, or what values you wish you were honoring then.

Pivotal Moments and Your Values

When we are faced with pivotal moments, we are forced to make decisions; those decisions reveal something about our core values. Document them.

Significant moment: _____

_____

_____

What was happening? _____

_____

_____

_____

_____

_____

What values were you honoring at the moment? _____

_____

_____

_____

_____

_____

_____

_____

What values do you wish you were honoring at the moment?

_____

_____

_____

_____

_____

_____

The second way to articulate your core values is to look at your favorite characters (fictional and/or nonfictional). I started this chapter talking about Superman; I did that because he is my favorite superhero and someone I have identified with since I was a kid. My moving around all over the world often made me feel like an alien and an immigrant. I often wondered which part of my identity to reveal, because I related to a lot of things. At the same time, I also wanted to do something bigger than myself and speak up for others—so when I came across Superman's comics, I thought I was looking at a mirror image, because Superman also believed in the best of humanity despite living in a cynical world.

I identified with his desire to do the right thing, even when it was difficult, as much as I related to Nelson Mandela's values of equality, courage, and service and Oprah Winfrey's values of perseverance, generosity, and spirituality.

Knowing why you admire the people you do gives you insight into your core values.

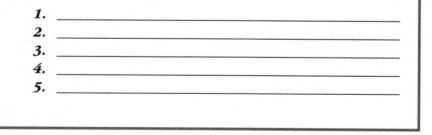

Who Are Your Heroes?

Make a list of five people you admire in the fiction or nonfiction world and write out what values you admire the most from them and why.

1. _____
2. _____
3. _____
4. _____
5. _____

Between the two exercises, you should have a pretty extensive list of values. Group all these core values together into related themes.

After you have grouped these values together, cut your list down to your five values. Underneath each value, write out why it is one of your core values and how it makes you who you are. Then list out a series of action steps that outline how you will live out your values on a daily basis.

Five Core Values

Core Value 1:
Why is it important to you?

_____

_____

_____

_____

_____

Action plan to live out this value on a daily basis:

_____

_____

_____

_____

_____

Core Value 2:
Why is it important to you?

_____

_____

_____

_____

_____

(Continued)

Action plan to live out this value on a daily basis:

_____

_____

_____

_____

_____

_____

Core Value 3:
Why is it important to you?

_____

_____

_____

_____

_____

Action plan to live out this value on a daily basis:

_____

_____

_____

_____

_____

Core Value 4:
Why is it important to you?

_____

_____

_____

_____

_____

Action plan to live out this value on a daily basis:

_____
_____
_____
_____
_____
_____

Core Value 5:
Why is it important to you?

_____
_____
_____
_____
_____
_____

Action plan to live out this value on a daily basis:

_____
_____
_____
_____
_____
_____

Use your top five core values to come up with a personal core value statement.

_____
_____
_____
_____
_____
_____

If you need any help picking out a list of values, feel free to use the following samples as a guideline to naming some.

A

Abundance, Acceptance, Accountability, Achievement, Advancement, Adventure, Advocacy, Agency, Ambition, Appreciation, Assertiveness, Attractiveness, Authenticity, Autonomy

B

Balance, Belongingness, Benevolence, Beauty, Boldness, Brilliance

C

Calmness, Caring, Challenge, Charity, Cheerfulness, Cleverness, Community, Commitment, Compassion, Conformity, Cooperation, Collaboration, Connection, Consistency, Continuous learning, Contribution, Courage, Creativity, Credibility, Curiosity

D

Daring, Decisiveness, Dedication, Dependability, Diligence, Discipline, Diversity

E

Efficiency, Empathy, Encouragement, Enthusiasm, Equality, Ethics, Excellence, Excitement, Expertise, Exploration, Expressiveness

F

Fairness, Family, Fitness, Friendship, Flexibility, Forgiveness, Freedom, Fun

G

Generosity, Grace, Gratitude, Growth

H

Hard work, Happiness, Health, Honesty, Hospitality, Humility, Humor

I
Impact, Inclusiveness, Independence, Individuality, Innovation, Inspiration, Integrity, Intelligence, Intimacy, Intuition

J
Joy, Justice

K
Kindness, Knowledge

L
Leadership, Learning, Love, Loyalty

M
Making a difference, Mindfulness, Motivation

N
Neatness, Nurturing

O
Optimism, Open-mindedness, Order, Originality

P
Passion, Patience, Performance, Perseverance, Persistence, Personal development, Peace, Perfection, Playfulness, Pleasure, Popularity, Power, Professionalism, Preparedness, Proactivity, Professionalism, Punctuality

Q
Quality

R
Recognition, Reciprocity, Relationships, Reliability, Resilience, Resourcefulness, Respect, Responsibility, Responsiveness, Risk taking, Romance

S
Safety, Security, Self-actualization, Self-care, Self-control, Selflessness, Sensuality, Serenity, Sexuality, Service, Simplicity, Skillfulness, Speed, Spirituality, Spontaneity, Stability, Strength, Success, Supportiveness

T

Teamwork, Thankfulness, Thoughtfulness, Traditionalism, Trust-worthiness

U

Understanding, Uniqueness, Usefulness

V

Valor, Versatility, Virtue, Vision, Vitality

W

Warmth, Wealth, Well-being, Wisdom, Work-life balance

Z

Zeal

These regular check-ins also allow you to make sure you're living in alignment with your core values, which ultimately allows you to live a life of awareness. It is important to note that as you grow and experience new things, your values will change, so I encourage you to regularly check in with your top five values and see if they need updating or realignment.

A good example of values changing as a result of environment is Derek Black, who was a former white nationalist. His father founded one of the largest racist websites, called stormfront. His godfather is David Duke, who was a Grand Wizard of the Ku Klux Klan. Derek's experiences and values started to change as he headed off to college and experienced the world through other people's lenses. He was forced to look inward and confront his core values and biases. Through that experience, he realized that he wasn't actually living in accordance with his values, and he made the decision to change that.

How Our Biases and Values Help Us Connect

Reflecting on both our biases and our core values are necessary habits to cultivate if we are going to make progress in connecting. They also help you maintain your sense of individuality while fostering your curiosity.

When you're more aware of who you are, you're less subject to your unconsciousness taking over. This helps you to avoid knee-jerk reactions, which can reveal our darker sides or our shadow sides.

Darker versions of ourselves appear when we don't live in accordance with our values. Our shadow sides are the sides of our personalities with aspects of ourselves that we don't like admitting to having. The more we adhere to our value systems, the better we become at setting boundaries and building connections. When we can't tell better stories of ourselves, our worse instincts take over because we externalize and project what we are not comfortable with.

It's important to realize that we are all flawed, because the more we accept ourselves as flawed, the more we'll be able to connect to others. Although we become more aware of our darker sides, let's not dwell on them. The Dalai Lama says in his book *An Appeal to the World* that the primary causes of war and violence are our negative emotions. He says we give too much space to them and too little space to our intellects and our compassion.

Our brains are neuroplastic. Neuroplasticity is the brain's ability to reorganize itself by forming new neural connections throughout life. This means that your brain can adapt. It will take intense focus but it is possible, and it happens every day. As you seek to improve your self-awareness, think about the words of Mahatma Gandhi: "Your words become your actions, Your actions become your habits, Your habits become your values, Your values become your destiny."

I'd like us to commit to living out our core values. I can't help but wonder what would happen if we regularly reflected on our actions and how they align with our values. Would you be happy with yourself?

The Role of Emotional Intelligence

I want to pause here to talk about emotional intelligence. Emotional intelligence (EI) or emotional quotient (EQ) is the ability to understand and manage your own emotions and those of the people around you. People with a high degree of emotional intelligence know what they're feeling, what their emotions mean, and how these emotions can affect other people.

According to Daniel Goleman, an American psychologist who helped to popularize emotional intelligence, there are five key elements to emotional intelligence:

1. Self-awareness: the ability to accurately recognize your emotions, strengths, moods, actions, and how these affect others around you.
2. Self-regulation: the ability to control your impulses, the ability to think before you speak/react, and the ability to express yourself appropriately.
3. Motivation: the drive and interest in learning and self-improvement. This typically involves goal-setting and follow-through.
4. Empathy: the ability to understand other peoples' emotions and reactions.
5. Social skills: the ability to pick up on social cues, maintain relationships, and find common ground with others.

The good news is that emotional intelligence can be learned and developed over time. You might feel uncomfortable at first but with practice and dedication, using it becomes a habit. It is essentially broken up into two components:

1. The capacity to be aware of, control, and express one's emotions (which we have just reviewed).
2. The capacity to handle interpersonal relationships judiciously and empathetically (which we discuss next).

4

Education of Environment

Now that you've done the hard work of understanding yourself, your thoughts, and why you think the way you do, it's time to educate yourself on the environments around you. It's easy to lose sight of the effect our behavior has on others, yet seeing our behavior through others eyes' is a critical part of becoming more self-aware.

How do you do that? By

- ◆ Learning how to collect and gather information.
- ◆ Becoming an active listener.
- ◆ Being an active part of your community.

Learn How to Collect and Gather Information

Let's start off with collecting and gathering information. I said earlier that my dad was a diplomat and that we moved often because of his job. By the time I was freshman in college, I had lived in five countries and four continents, and with every move, I observed my dad as he sought to understand his new environments and establish relationships.

I watched him try to maintain international relations with regard to issues of peace, war, trade, economics, culture, the environment, and human rights. I also observed as he sought to establish common ground with his colleagues, locally and internationally. His morning routine before he went to the office was to read the newspaper (back when we did that sort of thing), tune in to the BBC, then CNN, and then the local news stations.

I would ask him, "Dad, why do you do these things?" and he responded with this: "Akintayo, the world is bigger than you and if you want to succeed in it, you have to understand it."

> ## The world is bigger than you and if you want to succeed in it, you have to understand it.

He was basically trying to understand the differences around him and find the commonalities that existed within them. He was working on developing his cultural intelligence or his ability to relate and work effectively across cultures while trying to develop his emotional intelligence by understanding interpersonal relationships.

How Can You Apply This to Your Everyday Life?
Remember when you were identifying your biases as you were improving your self-awareness to acknowledge the cultures or groups of people you felt uncomfortable around? Now it's time to work through those feelings.

Finding Your Inner Sherlock

Take a look at the groups of people you're uncomfortable around and pay attention to what makes them smile, frown, and flock together.

Make note of all these things, and then put them aside and read about the history, culture, and current events surrounding the cultures you're investigating. As you start to do this, you'll start to begin the process of humanizing people who you usually feel uncomfortable around.

This is part of what I call **Finding Your Inner Sherlock**, or being able to observe, deduce, and conclude, based on your intuition. Sherlock Holmes, of course, is the most famous fictional detective in the world. Sir Arthur Conan Doyle's creation taught us the importance of noticing the smaller details and being present in order to see the bigger picture.

Let's get into how you can start becoming better at collecting and gathering information.

Record Your Observations and Findings Ethnography, as Webster's dictionary defines it, is the study and systematic recording of human cultures. Based on the biases you found you have, create a note-taking system that documents the sociocultural contexts, processes, and meanings within the cultural systems you're investigating. Here's a model I recommend:

> **Week 1:** Do one action within the week to learn more about the type of person you have a bias toward (read an article, book, blog, podcast, etc.).
>
> **Week 2:** Commit to learning more about someone in that group, either at work, in a professional network, or a social setting, and pay attention to your body language and communication going into the interaction, during the conversation, and after. Journal it.
>
> **Weeks 3 and 4:** Try to meet someone new to interact with, journal the interaction, and see if anything changed.

Continue to repeat this until it becomes a habit. If you don't want to do this by yourself, I encourage you to find accountability partners. You can do this at schools, workplaces, and in family gatherings. You might find yourself a bit frustrated during this exercise, but trust me when I say that discomfort means growth.

Acknowledge Your Senses I also recommend that, beyond your biases, you focus your attention on acknowledging your senses. You could work on any or all of the following senses: taste, sight, touch, smell, and sound. As you go about your day, you will find yourself encountering different people and different experiences. Record them in your journal this way.

Taste
What things did I taste today?

What did the things I tasted remind me of?

Sight

What things and people caught my eye? Why?

What clothes did the people I met today wear?

Who did the people I met look like? What was the color of their eyes? Hair?

What rooms did I walk into today and what did the room look like? What were the colors of the walls, furniture, ceilings, and floors?

Touch

What things did I touch today? What did they feel like?

What did the things I touch remind me of?

Smell

What things did I smell today?

What did the things I smelled remind me of?

Sound

What things did I hear today?

What did the things I heard remind me of?

What you'll start noticing in yourself is that you begin to notice patterns and come up with frames of references that are familiar to you. This will put things into perspective from a point of view you can understand. You will begin to build connections between what your senses feel and what you know. You'll start calling on memories you have had before, which will boost your drive to form connections in your environment.

Meditate   When I first heard about meditation, I thought it was some woo-woo tactic that was practiced by people who were out of touch with reality (an example of how my bias misinformed me based on limited exposure). However, as I started to study leaders like Oprah Winfrey and the Dalai Lama, I began to see how it helped them connect with people vastly different from them. After seeing this, I decided to give it another try. I downloaded a guided meditation app called Breethe and committed to meditating at least 10 minutes a day. I noticed that my focus and my memory improved, I was able to reflect on my day and journal recordings, and I had more emotional control.

As you incorporate meditation into your life while learning about your environment, I urge you to set an intention to connect with others and to imagine how you will react to various scenarios that could arise as you seek to understand your environment. This will help you to become more comfortable connecting across cultures as well as help you manage some of the discomfort that may arise as you're collecting and gathering information. The more you meditate, the more your day slows down. The more your day slows down, the more you become present. The more present you become, the more you notice. According to a Harvard study, about 47% of waking hours are spent thinking about what isn't going on. That means we spend close to half of our day being absent.[1]

Study Microexpressions While doing research for this book, I got to interview two of the leading body language experts in the world and founders of the Center for Body Language, Patryk and Kasia Wezowski. I wanted to learn more about microexpressions and how to read nonverbal body language. Microexpressions are facial expressions that occur within 1/25th of a second (see Figure 4.1).

FIGURE 4.1 Patryk and Kasia Wezowski Highlighting Different Microexpressions.

They are involuntary and expose a person's true emotions. According to Patryk and Kasia, even though body language varies significantly across cultures, microexpressions remain consistent across all known cultures.

Recognizing and interpreting microexpressions takes practice, but there are a few things you can start doing immediately to improve your skills. Listed below are what Patryk and Kasia suggest you can do to study microexpressions.

First, study the common microexpressions pictured in Figure 4.1 so you know the hallmarks of each. Disgust, for example, involves downturned lips, while people feeling contempt might show it by inadvertently pulling one side of the mouth up. Surprise and fear might look similar, but the latter emotion will cause people to pull their brows together.

Second, if you know you're about to visit or inter-act with another culture, educate yourself on the local body language—including masking techniques. YouTube is a great tool for this: Find videos of 10 executives from that culture and watch how they communicate.

Third, when you're in the moment, pay attention. You can't interpret microexpressions if you don't notice them. Don't make your counterpart uncomfortable with an unwavering stare. But do keep your focus on the face.

Fourth, listen to your intuition. When you notice a tiny facial movement, ask yourself: "What could that mean?" Humans are wired to subconsciously detect even the subtlest of emotional flashes, so your gut instinct may be correct.

You might also try to mimic the movement. When you repeat what you saw—whether it was a quick eyebrow raise or tightening of the lips, it not only gives you more time to think but also fires the mirror neurons in your brain, making it easier for you to associate the movement you saw with the correct emotion.

If you're still perplexed, start to exclude emotions. After memorizing the expressions in Figure 4.1, you should be able to quickly assess what the facial cue does *not* mean. For example, if you saw someone's eyebrows going down, you can exclude surprise, fear, or sadness—all of which are associated with raised eyebrows—and work from there.

If you're presenting to a crowd, as we were in Qatar, continue to scan the audience for microexpressions. Don't fixate on one negative look; instead, try to discern the sentiments of the majority.

Body language can be cultural, but emotions are universal. Microexpressions reveal someone's true feelings in a fragment of a second, so it pays to notice them and calibrate your behavior in cross-cultural interactions accordingly.[2]

To deepen your knowledge on the subject be sure to check out Patryck and Kasia's book, *The Micro Expressions Book for Business*.

As you start to do all this, you'll find yourself developing your critical thinking and deductive reasoning skills.

Become an Active Listener

Once you've incorporated collecting and gathering information into your routine, the second thing you can do to understand the environment around you is to become an active listener. Research shows that we only retain between 25 to 50% of what we hear.[3] It's no wonder a lot of us don't understand each other, right?

Just look at the divisions in today's climate:

Republican versus Democrat

Immigrant versus nonimmigrant

Nationalist versus Internationalist

DC fans versus Marvel fans

So much us versus them—from the mundane to the serious!

And I get it! We all like to think we are right, but are we willing to put all that pride aside?

I ask this because, if we are not willing to do this, we miss out on a chance to truly connect with the unfamiliar. A lot of us think we are listening but not many actively listen.

Active listening is:

◆ Listening to learn
◆ Listening to evaluate
◆ Listening to understand

LISTENING TO LEARN

Listening to learn starts with your intention. Tell yourself before you go into any listening session that your goal is to learn something new. Think of yourself as an interviewer. When you study the great interviewers like Oprah Winfrey and Graham Norton, you realize that what they are truly good at is asking open-ended and clarifying questions as opposed to leading questions. Their questions uncover emotions and open the door to storytelling. Storytelling is important because it allows people to tell you how *they* interpret the world. When people feel like you care about their stories, they become more comfortable.

These freeform types of questions provide opportunities for you to probe, which indicates interest and gives you insight into your audience's way of thinking. When you treat people the way *they* want to be treated and not how *you feel* they should be treated, you're onto something magical.

You're onto connection.

LISTENING TO EVALUATE

Listening to evaluate means critically examining what you've heard and seeking alignment. Once you find the alignment, frame your conversation by speaking to the values both you and your interviewee have. As you continue to ask open-ended questions, your goal should be to listen for personal feelings, opinions, or ideas on a particular subject. These will give you insight into the cultural significance of several things that are important to that person.

LISTEN TO UNDERSTAND

It takes a lot of concentration and determination to be an active listener, so ask questions, reflect, and paraphrase to ensure you understand the message. Remember, your goal here isn't to influence an outcome; it's to listen to what has been said and what hasn't. If you don't listen actively, then you could find that what someone says to you and what you hear can be amazingly different! Repeat what you heard verbatim. This is the easiest route, because the prospect will hear exactly what they just said and can either confirm their meaning or clarify their statement. Paraphrasing communicates to your audience that you care enough about what they said to put it in your words, which is empathy.

Be an Active Member of Your Community

The third thing that you can do to understand the environment around you is to be an active part of your community.

Pop quiz!

In your current community, do you know about the different types of people who live in it?

Do you know the socioeconomic makeup of it?

Do you know who your local and state leaders are?

Do you know how the same set of laws affects different types of people in your community?

If you don't, I encourage you to work on that. I encourage you to build your awareness of government, the community, and the authority and power of the environment you're investigating. This is about being informed about the world and rights of those around you.

Personally, I got my start with this type of behavior when my eighth-grade teacher, Miss McDonald, made us learn all the countries, capitals, and bodies of water in the world. When we asked her why this was important, she told us that if we wanted to be global citizens, we needed to understand the actual globe. She also said it would make us more curious.

In the spirit of her challenge to me back then, I'd like you all to challenge yourselves to build your curiosity muscles. Find out what's going on outside the walls of your comfort zone. Pick up a new language. Make a commitment to regularly travel to new communities. Volunteer in the inner cities. When you travel, don't just go to the tourist spots; enmesh yourself with the locals. At work or in school, join an affinity group or club that you know nothing about.

Curiosity is one of the most important traits you can develop. Here are some reasons why:

- It keeps your mind active rather than passive.
- It ensures that you become more observant of new ideas.
- It opens up new worlds and possibilities.
- It brings excitement into your life, which boosts your drive to learn.

Like my dad said, the world is bigger than you and if you want to succeed in it, you have to understand it.

Doing all this allows you to build empathy and become a perspective taker, which means you'll be able to temporarily suspend your own point of view in an attempt to view a situation as someone else might.

Notes

1. Steve Bradt, "Wandering Mind Not a Happy Mind," *Harvard Gazette*, 11 November 2010, news.harvard.edu/gazette/story/2010/11/wandering-mind-not-a-happy-mind/.
2. Kasia Wezowski, "How to Get Better at Reading People from Different Cultures," *Harvard Business Review*, 18 September 2018, https://hbr.org/2018/09/how-to-get-better-at-reading-people-from-different-cultures.
3. Ralph G. Stevens and Leonard A. Nichols, "Listening to People," *Harvard Business Review*, 1 August 2014, hbr.org/1957/09/listening-to-people.

5

Thinking Like a Sociologist

Everything I have described and discussed in this education section will prepare you to think like a sociologist. A sociologist's role is to study and understand social institutions, cultures, groups, organizations, and the way people interact across all these groups and institutions. Essentially, the role of a sociologist is to research, examine the way society is constructed around power structures, groups, and individuals, and examine the way multiple aspects of society behave and function. Following are different ways acting and thinking like a sociologist will help you become a better educator of self and environment—the big picture of different behaviors and the small picture of your role in society. I hope that this will help you develop the habit of seeing beyond the obvious.

Develop a Habit of Understanding Why Things Are the Way They Are

When sociologists observe something, they look beyond how people appear and act to understand why people behave the way they do by consistently looking for patterns. The late American-Austrian sociologist Peter Berger once said that, "even if one is interested only in one's own society, which is one's prerogative, one can understand that society much better by comparing it with others." Sociologists constantly search for context because they want to understand the evolution of things as well as the deeper meaning behind any person, problem, or situation. They don't accept the "it's just the way it is" narrative.

Translation: Don't rely on stereotypes to make your final decision about a person or group of people. Don Miguel Ruiz once said, "Don't make assumptions. Find the courage to ask questions and to express what you really want. Communicate with others as clearly as you can to avoid misunderstandings, sadness, and drama. With just this one agreement, you can completely transform your life." As you get to know a person or an environment, make an agreement with yourself that you will not make any conclusions based on your assumptions.

Study Melting Pots, Tossed Salads, and the Intersections in between Over Time

The melting pot theory is based on having a shared culture, having many facets of differing cultures within one single image or culture. Generally, there is one single unifying identity. The tossed salad concept implies that there are many diverse traits that make every place in a particular culture unique. Here, there is no single unifying identity. Some view assimilation as a force for unity, whereas others view it as an attack on identity. Some believe preserving heritage is a sense of pride and individuality, whereas others view it as a sign of stubbornness and division. A sociologist looks at these two concepts and the nuances in between before explaining their concepts to the world. This is particularly important because understanding the process of identity formation for individuals and societies over time plays a role in how institutions are shaped (more on this in Part II).

Thinking like a sociologist means challenging your assumptions, biases, and the complexities of who we are as individuals and the societies we build. There is hardly a one-size-fits-all process used when researching, asking questions, and observing. Approaching each study as if it is new and focusing on the context as opposed to the content of things is a habit that is regularly cultivated. You can do the same.

6

Applying LORA to Educate

As I discussed in the Introduction, **LORA** is my acronym for Listen, Observe, Reflect, and Act. I developed this model as a way to apply every concept I explain; what's shown here is for the Educate framework. It's both a summary and an action plan, so take out your journals and make note of all these.

Listen

Remember, as you're listening, be active. Listen to learn, evaluate, and understand. Make sure your instinct isn't to listen to confirm. Ways to listen to yourself are to learn about your biases and values. They define who you are, so constantly listen to them so you can acknowledge blind spots and growth opportunities. When you don't know your core values, you won't have the drive to connect. Being authentic leads to connection! True understanding of yourself sets you free. Remember, the first person you need to connect with in order to connect across cultures is yourself.

Observe

Observe your environments and the complexities of the characters around you. In yourself, observe your behaviors around people you're biased against. Observe your body language during those moments and make note of them. Observe your triggers. What gets them going?

In your current environment, who makes up your current group of friends? What do they believe? Who are the leaders? What are the demographics of your environment?

Reflect

This is very much about meditation and mindfulness. What habits do you need to unlearn and which ones do you need to develop? Some things to reflect on when you're working through your biases are as follows:

- ◆ How can I make myself a minority everywhere I have been?
- ◆ How can I understand the differences in my environment more?

When reflecting on your values, visualize yourself living in complete alignment with the best version of yourself. This person practices all your core values. How does it feel? Make this a daily practice. Continuously ask yourself:

- ◆ Does my lifestyle reflect my core values?
- ◆ What am I currently involved in that supports or furthers my values?
- ◆ Do I get as mad when insults are made against people I don't care for as I do when they're against someone I care about?
- ◆ Am I confident being myself? Why or why not?
- ◆ What do I do now that prevents me from being my authentic self? How can I break down those barriers?
- ◆ What is it that makes me who I am? What comes to mind when I think about who I am?
- ◆ In what moments is it particularly difficult to be myself? Why?
- ◆ Does who I am change depending on who I am with? Why or why not?
- ◆ What environments allow me to be completely comfortable being myself? Why?
- ◆ How often do I express my true feelings?

Wrap it up with the following affirmations:

- ◆ I have the courage to be myself at all times in all situations.
- ◆ I don't deny myself opportunities to grow into myself.
- ◆ Practicing my core values is a big priority for me.
- ◆ I act like myself at all times in spite of what fears I may feel.

These values are the foundation of your true self. We need be in alignment with what we truly value and who we are to be at peace. How are your values expressed in your everyday life? Reflect on these. The decisions and choices lead to how people connect to you.

Act

This is your plan of action. Based on everything you have listened to, observed, and reflected, how will you implement them on a daily, weekly, and monthly basis?

■　■　■

Once you educate yourself on who you are and your environment, you start to understand what will cause the other person to feel understood and that different perspectives matter.

Connect the Visible to the Invisible

We humans are tribal by nature, so we want to gravitate toward what we understand and what is familiar.

We fear what we don't understand because a lack of understanding represents a lack of control.

There is nothing necessarily wrong with similarities, but I want to encourage you all to reflect on how you react to differences.

Do you avoid them or make an effort to understand them?

I think if you make an effort to understand them, you'll find that we have a lot more in common than we initially think.

Diversity to me is much more than the color of our skin, our age, gender, or affiliations. It's also about the inside.

Essentially, true diversity is being able to connect the visible to the invisible.

How will you connect the visible to the invisible today?

When you don't see something or experience something, it's hard for you to acknowledge there's a problem, so awareness is key.

Part II
Don't Perpetuate

7

Don't Perpetuate Systems

Perpetuating contributes to systemic discrimination and inequalities for people and if you only learn and choose not to engage, you perpetuate.

—Tayo Rockson

I n the previous section, we discussed bias from an individual level. This section discusses how bias can operate on a systemic level. We will be looking at institutions and how to create a culture of belonging as opposed to one of separation. The institutions we will be diving into are the media, workplaces, and education. I believe these institutions dictate human behavior and policies that ultimately define culture and, by extension, society. The isms, negative stereotypes, and phobias that plague our world today prevail and get perpetuated when systems aren't being checked. We will dive into why that is so and how to safeguard against dangerous behaviors.

Sometimes, this section is met with dread and despair because fighting against a system can sometimes feel like a lonely journey. But if people created the systems we live in today, people can break down those same systems. My hope is that as you go through this section, you approach it with an open mind and a willingness to learn. I hope you prepare yourself to be comfortable with the uncomfortable, to be challenged, and, most important, I hope you will come away from this chapter ready to take action, because ignoring systemic problems hurts people.

Okay, let's get started on the dangers of perpetuating stereotypes.

Experiencing Stereotypes

To illustrate what can happen when you perpetuate stereotypes, I'll tell you two stories. Here's the first. Shortly after I graduated from college in 2011, I was asked to be part of a wedding in Lubbock, Texas, as a groomsman. Being a groomsman meant that I had to know the lay of the land, so I made sure I was at my most charming self. I greeted everyone, I met with the families, and I made eye contact with the pastor, but I couldn't help but notice that he kept giving me a curious look. I had noticed it as soon as I walked into the church, so I eventually walked up to him to ease any potential awkwardness.

I introduced myself and he did the same. He told me his name and asked me where I was from. I responded that I was from Nigeria and he clutched his wallet and said, "I better hide my credit cards" in a joking manner. I just stared at him and paused briefly to try and understand why he did that, then I figured out that he was referring to the stereotype that Nigerians sometimes get as credit card scammers impersonating princes. I was livid, but you wouldn't have been able to tell, because I just laughed it off. Unfortunately, the pastor was not done with me being the object of his amusement. He went on to tell the people around me that he was surprised that a Nigerian like me was so well dressed and eloquent—so much so that by nighttime, stories of "the black kid from Nigeria" had made their way to the extended family members of the groom and bride, and after I gave my toast at the rehearsal dinner, I was interrupted by an older white lady who felt the need to thank me as she grabbed my hand.

Caught off-guard, I asked her what she was thanking me for. She said that she was proud of me for not being like "those rappers on TV who have their hair braided and wear du-rags and have gold teeth." She said I represented a proper gentleman.

I just smiled at her and just nodded, once again feeling caught off-guard. Between the pastor playing to a dumb and untrue stereotype about Nigerians and this lady feeling the need to thank me for being myself, I felt dehumanized. But the night *still* wasn't done with ignorant comments.

To make matters even stranger, one of the other groomsmen felt the need to keep saying the word "nigga" around me and pointing to me as he sang along to a Drake song.

He had jokingly called me nigga before, as a way to ingratiate himself with me, I guess. I had told him then that I didn't find that word funny or appreciate being called that. Evidently, he didn't care, and on that dance floor, I couldn't be bothered to react anymore because I didn't want to ruin my friend's wedding. What I actually wanted to do was to give him a piece of my mind and who knows what else, but I took a deep breath, shook my head at him, and moved to another portion of the dance floor. In my head, I had weighed the pros and cons of reacting the way I wanted to and ultimately decided against it because I did not want to perpetuate the stereotype that many of the people there already had of black people. I didn't want to be the "angry black man."

Something about being pointed out as a nigga after being made fun of for being Nigerian and then being thanked afterward for not being a rapper while having to remain calm so as not to ruin my friend's wedding felt unfortunately familiar and reminiscent of my college days, which leads me to my second story.

When I first came to the United States for college in 2007, I was this 17-year-old freshman (or first-year student, for my non-American readers) with a mostly American accent, due to the time I spent in an American International school during my formative years. So, when I told people that I was Nigerian, they would not believe me because they had a different idea of what an African should look like.

I would then ask them what an African does look like, and they would retort with something like "You should be blacker and your English, it's too good! You speak it better than a lot of my friends."

I would then respond with asking them if they realized that Africa is a large continent with people that have different pigmentations. Furthermore, we are a continent of 54 countries, some of which were colonized by the United Kingdom, hence my English.

But they weren't done. They'd ask:

Did you live in a hut? **Nope**

Do you have cars? **Yes**

Did you sleep with monkeys growing up? **No, NO, NO, NOT A THING!**

And then, out of nowhere—I remember this vividly, like it was yesterday—some guy upon hearing that I was Nigerian extended his two hands as if he were carrying something imaginary and starting belting out, *"Nants ingonyama bagithi Baba Sithi uhm ingonyama Nants ingonyama bagithi baba Sithi uhhmm ingonyama Ingonyama Siyo Nqoba Ingonyama Ingonyama nengw' enamabala."*

This dude was straight-up doing *The Lion King*! I couldn't believe it and he had the nerve to laugh.

UnFREAKINGbelievable.

I looked at him, shook my head, and said something to the effect of, wrong region bro. I'm from Nigeria, which is in West Africa, and *The Lion King* was based in East Africa.

Then he began to make clicking noises with his mouth and, again, I had to correct him and tell him that that was the wrong region. The clicking noises he was making were made by the Xhosa tribe in South Africa. I am from the Yoruba tribe in Nigeria, which, once again, is in West Africa.

Again and again people would do things like these in jest or out of sheer curiosity.

The Danger of Perpetuating Stereotypes

Initially I was mad, of course, but then I started to see that 90% of the people asking me these questions were genuinely curious. This insight made me shift my perspective. I began to get less mad and to use those moments as educational opportunities. These experiences also gave me insight into a couple of things:

◆ Many of us reinforce stereotypes on a regular basis with jokes.
◆ Many of us trivialize stories of identity that are important to people we may not come into regular contact with.

What my collegemates and the people at the wedding were doing when they were making those microaggressive statements to me, knowingly or unknowingly, was perpetuating stereotypes. They were translating pieces of information they had received growing up or in the media and using me as a guinea pig to test out all the jokes they had heard about.

But what happens if a kid sees someone they respect or look up to doing that?

Hmmm ... seriously, what happens?

Chances are that kid then goes on to do the same thing to his or her circle of influence and the cycle of false narratives begins. This is a *very* hard and potentially *dangerous* cycle to break once it starts going. The narratives manifest themselves as revisionist history and fake news. I will discuss those later in this section but, before that, I want to talk about five concepts: identity, privilege, power dynamics, equality, and equity. An understanding of these five concepts will help paint the picture of how and why these dangerous systems are perpetuated.

8

Identity

Largely concerned with the two questions "Who am I?" and "What does it mean to be who I am?," **identity** relates to our basic values that dictate the choices we make (e.g., relationships, school, career). We discussed this largely in Part I, but when you go back to the two stories I started Part II with, you can see how institutions having incomplete stories of people can lead to a lack of opportunities as well as a negative perpetuation cycle.

The problem persists when institutions think of identities as one-dimensional rather than their intersectional characteristics. Identities are intersectional because they include race, gender, religion/spirituality, socioeconomic status, ethnicity, sexual orientation, and other dimensions that describe groups of people. The basic principle is that we all have multiple identities.

Revealing My Identities

My multiple identities, for example, include me being a Nigerian, a third-culture kid, a speaker, a consultant, a writer, a podcaster, a brother, a man, and a son. Taken separately, each of these unique aspects of who I am don't paint the full picture of my identity. Only when you sum up these aspects do you get close to my total identity.

As a Nigerian, I identify as a member of the Yoruba tribe, a West African, and an African. I proudly support my national soccer team and I generally root for Nigerians all over the world. I am filled with a tremendous amount of pride when I see people like Giannis

Antetokounmpo or Chimamanda Ngozi Adichie do well; same thing when I see Trevor Noah kill it with his career. We share a common African heritage.

A **third-culture kid**, or TCK, is someone who spent the formative periods of their lives outside of their parents' cultures. As a TCK, I live in intersections, which means I identify with many cultures simultaneously or at any given time. I could go from the extremes of not being seen as Nigerian enough or black enough or man enough, depending on the culture I am in, to being able to be friends with multiple people because of my background and ability to adapt. I have essentially been a **hidden immigrant** my whole life, someone who is able to look and sound pretty much like everyone else in their "home" country but, due to a TCK upbringing or other extensive overseas living, is not quite as native as the natives.

As a speaker, consultant, writer, and podcaster, I am constantly researching different cultures, studying human behavior, and sharing information based on my findings, so my identity can appear as activist, thought leader, guide, or storyteller, depending on who I am working with.

As a brother, man, and son, I have responsibilities to my family as well as how I show up in society to promote healthy masculinity.

Making Assumptions about Other People's Identities

We limit others by telling limited stories of who they are. In other words, we miss out on a chance to truly connect with others, because stories create connection pathways between multiple types of people as well as different emotions that lead to empathy. Charles Horton Cooley once said, "I am not what I think I am. I am not what you think I am. I am what I think you think I am."

Let's get better at not only telling full stories of people but also creating safe spaces for multiple identities.

Institutions need to create a sense of belonging that allows for multiple identities to coexist. Otherwise, they will miss out on noticing the shame, guilt, and sometimes trauma people have from having to hide parts of themselves.

I encourage institutions to go through the following series of questions with everyone they serve so as to know how to show up.

Discovering Other People's Identities

What are your multiple identities?

_____

_____

Are there any aspects of your identity you wish could be expressed more? Why?

_____

_____

_____

_____

What is your full name?

_____

How is it pronounced?

_____

Does it have a meaning?

_____

Do you know the ethnic origins of it? If so, what are they?

_____

_____

What makes you you?

_____

_____

_____

_____

List the places you have traveled to or lived that have had an effect on you and why.

_____

_____

_____

_____

Insiders versus Outsiders

When you allow full expression of self within your institution, you create spaces for connection and you create a sense of belonging. You also guard against in-groups and out-groups. An in-group is a group you are part of (genetically, socially, institutionally, culturally, or ideologically), whereas an out-group is a group you aren't part of. A lack of awareness of these will fuel separation and create insider-outsider dynamics.

What happens when insider and outsider dynamics occur?

Insiders are those who feel support, stability, and security from being in a group, who feel like their skill sets are optimized, and who feel that their contributions are valued.

Outsiders are those who want to have a sense of identity and understand that their contributions are not always valued, which typically leads to suboptimization of their talents or identity.

Basically, insiders sometimes aren't aware of the advantages they enjoy and continue to do things that are in their best interests and outsiders don't want to be perceived as complainers or agitators so they go back and forth internally with how they should interact or react.

Let me illustrate this concept of insider-outsider dynamics with an analogy. Consider what the world is like for left-handed people. Almost everything, including seats, utensils, scissors, and sports equipment, is designed for right-handed people. Right-handed people don't think about this because it doesn't affect them, but the minority group of left-handers must deal with it daily.

Just because you don't experience something doesn't mean that others don't. That's why it's so important to start with knowledge of self and your environment so you know how to stop behaviors that unintentionally exclude people.

A sense of belonging is something we all want to feel, so consider whether you are robbing people of that feeling. Remember, if you're part of the problem, you can be part of the solution. How are you allowing different identities to feel safe and be expressed in your institution? Does being different lead to people being ostracized in your institution? Can people bring their whole selves to your institution? Let's stop looking at groups of people as monoliths.

9
Privilege

So what exactly is privilege? **Privilege** is a special right, advantage, or immunity granted or available only to a particular person or group of people. This term has caused a lot of discomfort for many people, because sometimes some people feel that they are being blamed for something and other times, some people feel like they have to take on guilt and shame of some shape and form. Here's the thing, though: It isn't about that. It is about acknowledging and dealing with the societal, political, and institutional discrimination that plagues our world today. Your privilege can be your superpower if you use it to break down the cycles of oppression that exist today and become an ally. If you recognize your privilege and act on the influence it has, you can create a more connected world because your group is treated as the standard, while other groups are compared to yours.

One more thing: It is entirely possible to be privileged and oppressed at the same time. We'll tackle that idea later; first I want to address the following privileges: class, able-bodied, education, gender, gender identity, passing, racial, religious, sexuality, and citizenship.

Types of Privilege

Take a look at the following types of privilege and see which one(s) you identify with. If you have privilege, you have an opportunity to create more access systematically.

Class privilege: This is privilege relating to your social class or standing in society. Your standing in society is determined by several factors like income, occupation, and education level. These have a lot to do with your access to money and the opportunities that come from money in relation to others. The privilege comes from both your economic status and social class, which provide greater access to institutions like media, politics, education, and workplaces.

Able-bodied privilege: Gregor Wolbring describes able-bodied privilege as a "set of beliefs, presences and practices that produce—based on abilities one exhibits or values—a particular understanding of oneself, one's body and one's relationship with others."[1] It has to do with the benefits gained from being able-bodied. Some of the benefits are visible and some are hidden. The result is the false belief that "normal" human beings are the ones who can see with their two eyes, stand on their two feet, have two arms, 10 fingers, and don't have any mental illness. Here are some examples of what able-bodied privilege looks like:

1. Being able to use public transportation without much difficulty.
2. Being able to go into buildings without worrying about whether there's an accessible entryway or if the elevator is working.
3. Being able to go into buildings or make plans without worrying about accessibility, fatigue, or pain.
4. Not having to deal with uncomfortable glances from onlookers or being judged by others about your ability to do work.
5. Being able to wear clothes, feed yourself, cook, walk, or breathe by yourself.
6. Being able to go to public places without having to worry about accessible bathrooms or parking spaces.
7. Being able to drive yourself comfortably.
8. Not having to deal with people making ridiculous assumptions about what you can and can't do.

Education privilege: This is the ability to pursue and receive an education, should you wish to go that route, from trained and adequately compensated teachers. According to the UNESCO Institute for Statistics, 263 million children and youth are out of school globally.[2] Without access to education, opportunities decrease and when opportunities decrease, access to other privileges decreases as well. Access to higher education confers with it a number of privileges; so does your perceived credibility from a large part of society, fair or not.

Gender privilege: This is when opportunities are skewed toward one gender over another. An example of this would be the patriarchy we see today, evidenced in various parts of the world by the overrepresentation of men and their access to opportunities.

Gender identity privilege: This has to do with the ability to freely express yourself in any gendered term you identify with without having to worry about pushback, repercussions, discomfort, or judgment.

Passing privilege: This has to do with an ability to appear like a member of a more privileged group. An example of this would be in the past, when light-skinned people were able to pass as white in historically segregated times and therefore could share the privileges of a group that possessed more power. Passing privilege has also been used among members of the same ethnicity, one example being the Brown Paper Bag Test in African-American history. This was a form of racial discrimination practiced within the African-American community by comparing an individual's skin tone to the color of a brown paper bag. The test was reportedly used as a way to determine whether an individual was entitled to certain privileges. Those with a skin color that matched or was lighter than a brown paper bag were allowed admission or membership privileges. The test is a form of colorism or discrimination based on skin color.

Racial privilege: This is when things are set up systematically against members of different races, which means that power, money, opportunities, and influence are afforded to one racial group at the expense of another. It is important to note that even though race is a social construct, racism is real and systems that fuel racism have been instituted throughout history. They existed in the past and continue to exist today.

Religious privilege: This is the privilege earned from being part of the dominant and accepted religion in any given culture or society. An example of this is how in some countries, it appears to be safer to be a Christian than a Muslim and how in other countries it is vice versa. This of course is not only experienced among members of these two religions. It happens all over with different religions, as well as with different denominations within the same religions.

Sexuality privilege: This is the privilege assigned to people who identify as heterosexual. We live in a heteronormative world, which means that most people assume that heterosexuality is the norm or default sexual orientation. This means that members of the LGBTQ community are constantly put in positions of having to "come out." There are also many places in the world that are unsafe for members of the LGBTQ community.

Citizenship privilege: This one is very tricky, but it is real. It affects how you can move in the world. Sometimes, it is easier for people from certain countries to obtain visas or gain entry into some countries than others. You could find yourself not enjoying certain privileges by virtue of being an immigrant, international student, or holding your DACA card.

All these privileges are not meant to make anyone feel bad at all. They are just what they are—the reality of our world today. In fact, I'm sure that as many of you read through this list of privileges, you found yourself at an intersection of benefiting from some of the privileges as well as missing out on others. Like I said earlier, it is entirely possible to be simultaneously privileged and oppressed.

However, what we decide to do with our privilege can directly impact how we connect with our world. It is imperative that individuals and institutions acknowledge the privileges that exist around them and use their powers to create equitable opportunities. It's like the great Audre Lorde once said: "You don't have to be me in order for us to fight alongside each other." We are more unaware of what we have than what we don't have. The sooner we acknowledge our "haves" as institutions, the more bridges we will build.

All this leads me to power dynamics.

Power dynamics are the way different people or different groups of people interact with each other and where one of these sides is more powerful than the other. How often do you notice power dynamics around you, and what do you do about them?

Observing Power Dynamics

On a weekly basis, document all the power dynamics you notice as individuals and institutions. Then, write out what action you take or refuse to take. The more action you take by educating yourself and engaging, the less disconnection you will witness.

Equality and Equity

Equality is treating everyone the same way and **equity** is giving everyone what they need to be successful. There's a misconception that treating everyone the same is fair, but that's not true. Equal treatment can actually remove identity and differences in some instances because it assumes that everyone starts from the same starting ground. As you gain understanding of privileges and power dynamics, you can understand why it would make sense to, for example, provide extra lessons for people who don't speak English as their first language in classrooms or build gender-nonconforming bathrooms for gender-nonconforming people. You would understand why it's important to create opportunities for non–able-bodied people to enter your building just as much as you do for able-bodied people.

In the scenarios above, equality was providing education, bathroom, and a building, respectively, while equity was making sure different types of people could feel comfortable being themselves in those institutions. Both are necessary, but there's a subtle difference: The goal is give people the same opportunities to succeed, regardless of individual differences. Another one of the amazing late Audre Lorde quotes illustrates this: "It is not our differences that divide us. It is our inability to recognize, accept, and celebrate those differences."

As an institution, do you create opportunities to incorporate all the different types of individuals you have responsibility for? Are you changing the systems of privilege and power dynamics so that historically underrepresented and disadvantaged groups now have a voice?

Barriers to Connection

The two biggest barriers to connection are fear and ignorance, and right now, some are using media to promote ignorance and monger fear, and because this promotes oppression, we need to make sure that those "some" don't succeed. Oppression is having to deal with being treated unfairly because of who you are. It's having to deal with microaggressions. It's having to deal with systems and institutions working against you no matter what you do. So not working to dismantle these institutions that promote oppression actually means that you're pro-disconnection.

An understanding of identity, privilege, power dynamics, equality, and equity is imperative for institutions and individuals to understand in order to foster safe environments for connecting across cultures.

Privilege. You don't see it so you don't feel it. You don't live it so you don't know it. Understand your privileges and the gaps they can create.

Next, let's dive into the institutions.

Notes

1. Gregor Wolbring, "The Politics of Ableism," *Development* 51 (2008): 252–253.
2. "263 Million Children and Youth Are Out of School," *UNESCO UIS*, 27 April 2017, uis.unesco.org/en/news/263-million-children-and-youth-are-out-school.

10
The Media

The media has played a huge role in shaping culture for many, many reasons. Its footprints are in all our lives: How we receive information. How we report information. How we see others. How we engage and how we learn about the world.

Whether we know it or not, virtually all of us interact with the media on a daily basis, so it makes sense to truly examine the role it plays in our lives.

The media can also be used as a tool for negative perpetuation if we are not careful.

Negative perpetuation happens because of three reasons: ignorance, incomplete stories being circulated, and fake news.

Let's take a look at the 2016 U.S. presidential election. On one side, we had the Republicans, and on the other, we had the Democrats. We even had a large group of people who didn't identify with either, so there was lots of dissension in the ranks. However, one of the things that all sides could agree on was that there was a lot of false information, or fake news, going around. There are several studies that show that thousands of people fell for the allure of completely fabricated news. In fact, Google had to banish more than 200 sites from its AdSense network and change its news feed algorithm to combat fake news.

Not only that, there were troll farms being set up in multiple places with the deliberate goal of spreading disinformation. A **troll farm** is an organized operation of many users who may work together in a "factory" or from different places across a distributed network to generate online traffic aimed at affecting public opinion and to spread misinformation and disinformation. These highly organized propaganda factories infiltrated several forms of media to incite division, violence, and influence election results.

There's a whole industry built on clickbait news, so we need to be better fact checkers and be careful about where we get our information. It is our responsibility to be engaged as global citizens and, more important, to accept the idea that multiple perspectives can be right.

Fake news, as I said earlier, leads to incomplete stories and watered-down history lessons. If we don't address these, they have the potential to reinforce dangerous beliefs and create **echo chambers** (an environment in which a person encounters only beliefs or opinions that align with their own, so that their existing views are reinforced and alternative ideas are not considered).

We have to fight this because lies like these can be weaponized into dangerous messages of propaganda and division.

In the following chapters, I will be addressing this idea, as well as three aspects of media that we can improve on today to improve connection across divides: journalism, platforms, and entertainment.

Journalism

Henry Anatole Grunwald, the former managing editor of *TIME* magazine, once said that "journalism can never be silent: that is its greatest virtue and its greatest fault," and I tend to agree. What journalists say or don't say impact our world for better or worse. I'd like for us to get back to independent, trusted journalism, one that is devoid of outside influence or motivated solely by profit. At its best, journalism should be used for investigating the truth of issues and/or telling stories of the world as it is. Some would say that journalism is a voice for the voiceless. At its worst, journalism can be used as a **propaganda** machine that pumps out biased or misleading pieces of information used to promote or publicize a particular political cause or point of view. Journalism needs to practice engagement, representation, transparency, and partnership. Let's get into what I mean exactly.

JOURNALISM CANNOT FORGET ENGAGEMENT

I first heard of engaged journalism while interviewing Emmy award–winning innovation strategist and the inaugural Chair in

Journalism Innovation and Civic Engagement for the University of Oregon's School of Journalism and Communication, Andrew DeVigal. DeVigal believes that journalists shouldn't just think of the public as "audiences" and "experts." Rather, they should also think of the public as collaborators. I like this because this promotes humanization and respect. We discussed the current nature of media and what seems to be missing from it. It seems like there is a competition between networks to have the loudest talking heads who say outlandish things for shock value and ratings (obviously, not all networks are like that).

It seems like we have deviated from including the public in the narrative, due to the cash-strapped and resource-strapped nature of the industry, where clicks and volume of stories have taken precedence over authentic storytelling. What journalism misses out on in this process is building relationships with the audience it serves. We need to promote relational engagement over transactional engagement. The good thing is that this doesn't just apply to journalists—it applies to all of us. Figure 10.1 is what DeVigal calls the Continuum of Public Engagement in Journalism.

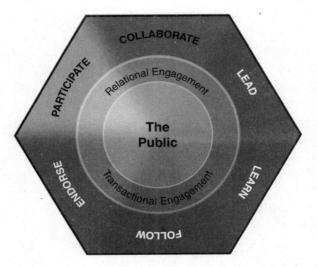

Figure 10.1   The Continuum of Public Engagement in Journalism by Andrew DeVigal.
Source: Reprinted with the permission of Andrew DeVigal.

Shown on one side of the continuum are learn, follow, and endorse. These are transactional types of relationships because you give something to a publisher that they give back to you in a transactional way. It's usually a one-sided relationship.

To learn, you could read articles or blogs or listen to podcasts. When you follow, you are deciding to subscribe to a newsletter or news feed and when you endorse, you're buying a membership or choosing to share a story with your audience.

On the other side of the continuum are participate, collaborate, and lead. These are relational forms of engagement.

To participate, you could submit questions to entities that can answer questions about your environment or you can attend community gatherings that include people who disseminate information around you, like reporters, journalist, statisticians, anthropologists, and so on. These community gatherings can be city hall or town hall meetings. Newsrooms can do this by organizing their own meetings and engagements with the public so as to facilitate open dialogue. They can discuss what should be covered and what should be the focal stories. You essentially are participating in your local information ecosystem. Can you trust the data and information that describe the world around you and can you participate in producing it?

To collaborate, you could accompany reporters and contribute to news stories. Jennifer Brandel, the cofounder and CEO of Hearken, a platform that helps journalists do work that better reflects the information needs and desires of their audience, has a great framework for this. Her platform cultivates questions from their audience of what they hadn't seen covered in the news. The Hearken team then curates the best questions that they believe would be of interest to the larger audience before putting those questions up for a public vote on their website. This puts the audience in the position of editor. The person whose question ultimately wins gets to accompany a reporter on some aspect of the reporting process. Hearken works with their audience to set the news agenda. *Brilliant!*

Although this might not be scalable or applicable to all journalism institutions, I believe elements of Brandel's model can be applied to every newsroom.

News organizations can also collaborate with each other on specific investigative series. We live in a digital world, so let's use those platforms to connect and collaborate.

To lead, you could join a news organization's community advisory board. If one doesn't exist, you could encourage your local news station to create a community advisory board so that they have feedback and there's the relationship built in to help tell representative stories. You could also form a local news cooperative by connecting with trusted members and representatives of your community. You can support a healthy information ecosystem in your community.

This last point is actually how I fell into media. I wasn't satisfied with the way news outlets covered stories of people like me, who constantly lived in between cultures, so I figured I would launch a podcast to create a platform for this underserved audience. What evolved was a community and ecosystem of people who started to feel seen, heard, and understood. As my podcast, *As Told By Nomads*, found an audience, I started getting requests to collaborate on projects in institutions, which ultimately let to my current career. My podcast, which is the freest thing, has ultimately created room to tell a wide range of stories. It has also allowed me to collaborate with my audience to get more representative stories. Everyone can do this on a micro or macro level. Focus on the connections you're making and how you can learn from different stories you learn and you'll find yourself telling more stories representative of our world today.

Ultimately, I believe the media is an institution that needs to be more collaborative when telling stories of the community. It needs to authentically include the public and communities into the process of journalism. You can't tell the story about the community without them. Like DeVigal says, "in our radically connected world, journalism has to be connected to the people and include the knowledge, insights and experience of the public to help tell the stories of the public."

Journalism can build relationships, especially when it represents underrepresented and underserved people. Diversify the coverage *and* the newsrooms. Create opportunities for these people to tell their stories. No one wants to be defined by others. The public needs to be media-literate and the media needs to be more community-literate. The future of journalism has to be collaborative for trust to be restored because it has been eroded—however, I don't believe that it has been eroded beyond repair.

Platforms Have to Acknowledge Their Power

Platforms like Facebook, Google, Twitter, and other social media platforms have a lot of power in the digital age. The very ecosystem that allows social media to connect people all over the world is the same one that allows disinformation to thrive. **Disinformation** is the dissemination of false information, rumors, hoaxes, or propaganda with the intent to mislead and influence public opinion. Various institutions, including governments and corporations, use this all the time. This isn't new but has intensified in recent years due to social platforms. Today it is becoming increasingly difficult for people to distinguish between real and fake information.

Take the unfortunate ethnic cleansing that started happening in Myanmar on August 25, 2017. More than 700,000 of the mostly Muslim country's Rohingya minority group fled the country because of systematic and organized attacks, rapes, and murders organized by the government. The Myanmar military used social media to heighten anti-Rohingya propaganda and incite these heinous crimes, thereby causing the largest forced human migration in recent history. People with knowledge of the campaign have said that hundreds of military personnel created troll accounts, news, and celebrity pages on Facebook and used these pages to create fake stories and spread false stories to both Muslim and Buddhist groups about impending attacks from the other side. These posts were being sent out at peak viewership times. Under the cover of popular pages, the military used Facebook Messenger to send warnings and spread rumors of Jihad attacks to the Buddhist groups. They sent different messages to Muslim groups about anti-Muslim protests. All these, as you can imagine, caused rampant sentiments of tension and uneasiness that positioned Myanmar's military to be the saviors.

Platforms can no longer pretend that they don't have a role in how people receive information. Leaders of these platforms have to decide if their services will be breeding grounds for extremism or tools for citizen journalism and connection. On his brilliant show *Patriot Act*, Hasan Minhaj said it best when he said that platforms are getting all the benefits of publishers with none of the risks.

If platforms are going to be used as publishers, they have to take ownership and clean up hate speech and troll farms being set up on their networks. If they don't, they risk feeding into systems of oppression, and systems of oppression are disconnectors. Feigning ignorance is no longer an option.

FAKE NEWS IS ENTICING

So why are we susceptible to fake news anyway? Because we don't promote a culture of reflection and research. We are programmed to be reactive. The juicier the gossip, the better the story. It's why sometimes tabloids sell out quickly despite the fact that they are selling lies. Once, at a store where I was buying some chewing gum, I saw two magazines placed next to each other: One had a headline proclaiming that Brad Pitt and Jennifer Aniston were getting back together and the other had a headline that basically said that Jennifer Aniston and her now ex-husband Justin Theroux were madly in love.

Which was true?

Was *any* of it true?

I have no idea. One of them could be true or they both could be lies, but the point is that these things sell. It's like CNN's Christiane Amanpour once said at SXSW, "we're in an existential moment right now. We are at a peril and risk if we don't know the difference between truth and lies ... because human beings actually kind of gravitate to something that sounds so extraordinary and then they want to share it."

We want to share something extraordinary and people with ulterior motives know this, so they manipulate this desire to connect and bond over gossip and they use platforms to disseminate information that is actually dangerous. This is called disinformation.

Couple this with the fact that, as I discussed in the first section of the book, we are all biased and our brains naturally want to be surrounded by comfort. This comfort seeks echo-chambered environments that confirm what we already think.

This all happens on individual, institutional, and societal levels.

On an institutional level, platforms should create systems that prevent bots from gamifying the system in such a way that fake news gets the most visibility. I get how adding advertising to viral posts is good for the platform on a financial level, but at what expense? Algorithms should be used to detect bots, identify fake news, and reduce financial incentives. This might be extreme, but I think platforms should consider instituting timers that range from 30 seconds to 2 minutes before sharing news. I believe that this will allow people to critically think about what they are sharing before they do it. Even instituting something that allows people to identify the source of news will limit disinformation and fake news.

VERIFYING WHAT'S TRUE AND WHAT'S FAKE

While the institution of platforms has to do better with policing their platforms by coming up with solutions to limit the disinformation, individuals have to do better about being fact-checkers.

So how do we get better at fact checking and verifying our stories? Here are some ways you can work on fixing the disinformation problem we have today:

- ◆ Pay attention to the domain and URL of the site you're getting your news from. Does it reflect the title of the page you're looking at?
- ◆ Read the About Us section. Who are the people behind the site? Can you find their bios to validate their work?
- ◆ Look up the quotes in your articles and validate them. If there are no quotes behind the claims made, validate.
- ◆ You could also use sites like snopes.com, FactCheck.org, PolitiFact, Media, and mediabiasfactcheck.com (which does a great job of disproving myths and legends as well as fact checking).

I also want you to honestly ask yourself these questions when you create content:

- How often do you fact-check your own content? Always, usually, sometimes, rarely, or never?
- How often do you verify other writers' work before sharing it? Always, usually, sometimes, rarely, or never?
- When citing a source, do you fact-check it? Always, usually, sometimes, rarely, or never?
- Do you have more than one trusted source for news? Yes or No?

As the election and Myanmar examples I provided earlier highlight, people are getting information from platforms like social media, and social media platforms are becoming news stations. What happens, though, when platforms meant to connect people become instruments of disseminating information? They become susceptible to governments and corporations potentially spreading propaganda or manipulating the media. After all, what platforms have done better than almost any institution in history is to bring people together, making it easy to form echo chambers using algorithms to insulate people from multiple perspectives.

What was once used for connection and reconnection is being used for disinformation. If we don't do a better job of addressing this, we create insider and outsider dynamics that promote the unintentional exclusion I discussed earlier, in which we have in-groups and out-groups.

We need to perpetuate a culture that promotes truth and transparency because **ignorance plus influence is dangerous and we risk promoting a cycle of ignorance through the media and platforms if we do not become better fact-checkers.**

Entertainment (Movies, Music, Books, and TV)

Here, I am basically referring to **pop culture** and its influence in our world today. Pop culture can be described as the mix of ideas, videos, images, attitudes, and perspectives that characterize a given culture and is loved and accepted by the mainstream population. It is culture that is considered popular and transmitted via the mass media.

For many, entertainment is often the introduction to other cultures. If you recall, in the first story I shared to start this section, I talked about how the older white lady thanked me for not being like other black men who had braids and gold teeth. It is clear that that she saw black people as a monolith and I was a shock to her. It is also clear that she had opened her mind to understand that people can wear whatever they want and that shouldn't be used to demean their status in society.

Entertainment is very important in today's world, so the gatekeepers of this institution have a big responsibility to make it representative of our world. Don't take my word for it; check out what the late great Stan Lee said about entertainment: "I used to be embarrassed because I was just a comic-book writer while other people were building bridges or going on to medical careers. And then I began to realize: entertainment is one of the most important things in people's lives. Without it they might go off the deep end. I feel that if you're able to entertain people, you're doing a good thing."

The more visible you make people, the more connected we'll be to our humanity. In the past few years, *Black Panther*, *Hidden Figures*, *Crazy Rich Asians*, and *Wonder Woman* have been released in the cinema. I saw each of them at least three times.

Why did I do that?

It's because I felt an enormous sense of pride. I felt this pride because the more I write, speak, podcast, and consult with companies and educational institutions, the more people I meet and the more I'm struck by how many people long to see themselves in stories; to see their identities and perspectives—their avatars—on the screen or in pages. They talk about not just being issues or think pieces to be addressed or icons for social commentary. They talk about their desire to simply be seen as people and heroes who get to do cool things in amazing worlds. I can't really explain it, but it's a beautiful experience to find yourself on the pages and screens of an entertainment channel. It's ... uh ... what's the word?

Magical!

When you experience this as a storyteller, you quickly realize that you have tremendous power and potential to literally empower people who have for many years felt like they didn't exist because their histories have been erased. You realize that you have the power to celebrate humanity in a beautiful and inclusive way. The great thing about this realization is that it's accessible to *all* of us if we decide to act, advocate, and support.

I remember watching *Black Panther* on the Thursday it came out—then the following day and the day after. With each viewing, I sat there smiling, laughing, and crying at random times. As a Nigerian, it felt so good to see my continent represented on the big screen and not in a patronizing way. I had waited for this day for such a long time and, in many ways, I didn't realize how much I needed it. The powerful thing about entertainment being used to tell inclusive stories can be summed up in one word:

REPRESENTATION

Superheroes are some of the first leaders that little kids gravitate toward, giving them a chance to imagine themselves doing amazing things. That was certainly the case for me with Superman, as I explained earlier. It's also why to this day I refer to myself as the African Superman. Yes, the African Superman.

But I digress …

The point is that since superheroes are one of the first way kids come into contact with leadership, let's make the heroes look more like them.

This does a few things.

It inspires confidence in underrepresented groups and gives them the ability to locate themselves in different stories.

It neutralizes bias.

It also offers us a chance to learn about new cultures and histories. More on this later when I talk about education as an institution, but let's consider the importance of a movie like *Hidden Figures*, which came out in 2016. In the movie, one troubling fact is brought to light—which is that Hollywood and our education systems have engaged in revisionist history for far too long. The fact that many people, including me, did not know about Katherine Johnson, Dorothy Vaughan, and Mary Jackson was troubling and embarrassing to me. Why didn't I know about these three ladies when I learned about Neil Armstrong, the first man on the moon? It speaks to how little we have used a platform as powerful as entertainment to tell stories of our world. Stories that have gotten us here. This goes for fiction and nonfiction stories alike.

Movies like *Wonder Woman*, *Crazy Rich Asians*, and *Black Panther* can inspire curiosity in all of us. Even though they are fiction, I believe that the deep-rooted sense of pride the protagonists had for their cultures is enough to get people more curious about the continents of Africa and Asia, as well as Greek/Roman mythology. When truly representative, entertainment can help bridge the chasms and divides that exist today, while celebrating diversity.

The media is an institution that plays a big role in how we receive information and see the world. Now, let's focus on the two institutions we spend most of lives in: educational institutions and workplaces. I'll start off with workplaces.

11

Workplaces

The main thing to strive for in workplaces is creating inclusive environments. There has to be a system in place that allows for multiple identities to exist safely while making sure that power dynamics and privileges don't infringe on the rights of others. On top of this, leaders in workplaces need to make sure that equality and equity exist, which requires courageous leadership, open-mindedness, and constant awareness. As a leader in your workplace, you should know what is important to all the stakeholders in your company and why.

Workforce diversity often includes the clear differences you see, such as ethnicity, race, religion, gender, age, national origin, and sexual orientation. Besides this, workforce diversity also includes the obvious traits, including the subtle differences that generally register with us unconsciously, for example, appearance, socioeconomic status, accent, marital status, language, and educational background. We all have something that makes us special, some unique ability or talent we bring to the table that differentiates us from other employees and our colleagues.

According to Deloitte, diversity has become increasingly important in today's political, economic, and global business environment, and the number of executives who cite inclusion as a top priority continues to rise.[1]

In an increasingly competitive marketplace, companies cannot afford to handle any activity or carry any extra weight that doesn't assist them in succeeding. So how does having a diverse workforce help in achieving a company's goals? There are several tangible benefits that a company can gain from having a diverse workforce, aside from just good-faith efforts and attaining legal compliance. In fact, as markets expand worldwide, being able to understand and reach out to the specific needs of every individual from other regions and cultures will be paramount. A trained multicultural and talented employee base gives companies that major advantage.

I believe that diversity and inclusion in the workplace should be approached with a top-down, bottom-up strategy. Engaging your employees at all levels is one of the most effective ways to reach critical mass and communicate the importance of inclusion and diversity. Most times, employees are willing to join in the process but lack the confidence and understanding to take action.

Diversity and inclusion is often a topic of debate, but I hope that by the time you're done reading this, you'll be able to define and make a case for both and outline a clear plan of action to achieving true long-term inclusion in your workplace.

Let's begin.

The Connection between Diversity and Inclusion

First of all, let's articulate the difference between diversity and inclusion.

Diversity refers to demographic differences that distinguish one person from another. These differences may be observable or unobservable. Diversity goes beyond visible differences to include things we can't see. We have to be able to look beyond the surface level. Diversity takes into account many things like personality, communication, leadership style, learning styles, economics, culture, work styles, language, social, privilege, and education.

These are just some of the things behind your visible forms of diversity such as age, race, gender, and orientation. When you just look at the visible, you miss opportunities to know who people really are. True diversity links the visible to the invisible.

Inclusion is the action or state of including or of being included within a group or structure. Inclusion is the state of being that supports diversity. It enables diverse individuals and groups to function in ways in which differences are respected, gifts are valued, and everyone is welcome, regardless of their diversity.

Inclusion is involvement and empowerment, where the inherent worth and dignity of all people are recognized. Inclusion looks like increased participation in decision making:

- ◆ Access to information.
- ◆ Greater empowerment of employees to solve organizational problems and collaborative teamwork.
- ◆ Inclusion moves beyond acknowledging difference. It embraces it.

The best analogy I've heard about these two terms is that diversity is like a seed and inclusion is like the fruit. Most seeds don't make it to the fruit stage because they haven't been nurtured properly. And if they aren't nurtured properly, they won't blossom. So when leaders say they hired for diversity and it didn't work out, it's because the talent wasn't nurtured the right way. ***They most likely didn't feel included.***

Add to that biases, assumptions, fear, and lack of understanding and you have a very shaky foundation. Diversity isn't about tokenizing people or filling quotas. It's about leveraging differences and making all our differences work for us.

Achieving sustainable diversity and inclusion in the workplace is a fundamental part of the twenty-first-century workplace. Some of the numerous benefits include:

- ◆ Enhanced creativity
- ◆ Higher retention rates
- ◆ Improved communication
- ◆ Effective problem solving

Making the commitment to diversity and inclusion is the first step. Educating ourselves on how deep the commitment must be over time is a big undertaking. Understanding that the work is multilayered is also important. There is no checklist.

Now, let's talk about five ways you can achieve sustainable diversity and inclusion. I call these the five A's.

Let's start with the first A, Assess.

Assess

In this stage you're in preparation mode and taking inventory of what the current diversity and inclusion temperature is like in your company. **For anything to be sustainable, you need to understand why you're doing it in the first place.**

A lot of companies falter at this stage because they are being reactive and not proactive. They heard something bad happened at Uber, Starbucks, and H&M, and they just react.

As you're assessing, these are some questions you should begin to ask yourself:

- ◆ What is diversity to you?
- ◆ What do you want the future of your organization to look like?
- ◆ Do you view diversity as an asset or liability? Why or why not?
- ◆ As a leader, are you personally ready to take this on?
- ◆ What is the business case of diversity for your company?
- ◆ How will this benefit employees?
- ◆ How will this benefit stakeholders?
- ◆ Are you willing to use your company's resources to ensure the success of your plan?
- ◆ What types of relationships do you have right now and what types of relationships do you need to develop in order to make this a reality?
- ◆ What biases exist currently and how will you measure the biases in the future?
- ◆ What are the core values of your organization?
- ◆ Do you have safe spaces for people to have honest dialogue without being ridiculed?

Note: In this stage, you're assessing diversity not only for the economic case, but also for the morality case.

DIVERSITY AND INCLUSION IS EVERYONE'S RESPONSIBILITY

I'm sure you all will agree with me when I say that sustainable diversity and inclusion doesn't belong in the human resource (HR) silo, right?

It has to be a priority for leadership, HR, and all the stakeholders of the company. *Everyone* has to be involved; there has to be commitment from the CEO, executives, HR, mid-level managers, and employees across various business units. A lot of companies neglect the mid-level managers, but that's a mistake because they often have significant influence on establishing and implementing new policies. They are also usually involved the most with day-to-day interactions with workspaces and the majority of the employees. Speaking of employees, assess how they feel about speaking out and their pain points. Do they feel like they can express themselves?

Another area to assess would be with your suppliers and vendors. What messages are your suppliers and vendors sending and receiving about you?

Assess, Assess, Assess.

What about your community partners? How are you getting involved with things like scholarships/internships, summer programs, mentorship programs with at-risk people, cooperative programs with high schools, universities?

Assess, Assess, Assess.

Back to diversity being both an economic and moral compass priority. True diversity and inclusion occurs when it is operating from the head as well as the heart. The head is the business case and the heart is the emotional and psychological case. If you do this right, then you're able to create a situation where people are accepted for much more than what they look like, but for who they are.

Assess, Assess, Assess.

When I work with companies, we go into multiple ways to assess the current situation and, without fail, people are always surprised by what they discover about their company and employer brand. Assess to find out what you want your organization's future to look like and to find out what you need to do to make it happen. Assess so that you are not stuck in a reactive place all the time.

Arrange

This part is all about strategy. Here, you're determining the plans of action you need to implement in order to succeed. The first thing you need to do here is to align your diversity and inclusion strategy with the overall vision of the organization. Make sure that when you meet to discuss strategy, you're adding a diversity and inclusion component to all of your business units. Every person in the company should understand how their job adds value to the overall strategy of the company as well as to the diversity and inclusion goals. Execs, middle managers, supervisors, and team leads should constantly be asking the following question: **"How does what I do fit in with our diversity and inclusion strategy?"**

Adding it as a performance goal for management helps to hold leadership accountable.

FORMALLY COMMITTING TO DIVERSITY AND INCLUSION

At this stage, I also suggest a public declaration of next steps in the form of a diversity manifesto and then both a mission and vision statement should be crafted at the end of this exercise. You want these statements to speak to your company's values and the company culture you aspire to cultivate.

Creating a Diversity Manifesto

In your diversity manifesto, include the following:

- ◆ What diversity and inclusion practices mean to <Your organization>.
- ◆ The desired work culture and expectations at <Your organization>.
- ◆ Desired diversity goals of <Your organization> in the next one, two, and five years.
- ◆ A layout or equation for the percentage of compensation and bonuses that will be allocated to senior leadership directly related to diversity goals.
- ◆ The budget percentage that will be allocated to diversity goals.
- ◆ An evaluation system that will be used to grade diversity efforts.

(Continued)

◆ A requirement that every member of the leadership, talent acquisition, and HR teams will take at least one of the Implicit Association Test (IAT) tests.

The manifesto should also clearly state the following:

◆ <Your organization> accepts all differences and integrates all ideas.
◆ <Your organization> treats all employees with dignity and respect.
◆ <Your organization> promotes collaboration with others and building effective working relationships.

This is important because it shows the employees that there is meaningful intention from the senior leadership to improve upon the existing diversity and inclusion practices.

An organization's commitment to diversity and inclusion is reflected by the prioritization of resources allocated toward effectively implementing the company's strategic vision.

Prioritizing diversity and inclusion demonstrates to employees that theory is turned into practice and that <your organization> is a *pro*active organization as opposed to a *re*active one.

When people feel good about themselves and the organization, they perform better individually and as part of a team, resulting in an organization that performs better.

IMPLEMENTING A DIVERSITY AND INCLUSION STRATEGY

The other necessary ingredient in the arrangement stage is that you start to form the team that can implement this strategy. My recommendation is to form a diversity council that's representative of the company. You want it to include HR, leadership, marketing, operations, finance, and all the business units that exist in your company.

Remember that diversity and inclusion has to include **everyone** and be an active part of your organizational value.

You want the diversity council to be able to strategize and brainstorm solutions for the problems you have systematically. You're looking at loopholes in your current marketing, HR, and people policies.

Forming a Diversity Council

Here are some questions you can use to get the council started:

- What are your organizational values?
- How can you make inclusiveness a way of being in your organization?
- What are some suggestions and ideas for the marketing team?
- How will you implement more inclusive policies based on what you assessed?
- Which partners can you include in your efforts to make this happen?
- What are the advantages?
- What are the disadvantages?
- What is your employer brand?
- What programs will you launch to help with awareness?

Doing this serves a dual purpose. Not only does it inform your employees and the world about what you believe in, it also informs everyone of your commitment to achieving the vision you set.

As far as structure, here's one to consider:

The committee should appoint a diversity VP or leader, in addition to having your organization's leadership team representative. These two individuals would collaborate on ideas for the committee and can be accountable for guiding the committee, as well as tracking and reporting progress. In addition, the VP of diversity should report to the CEO every six months.

Recommendations for the Diversity Committee Purpose The diversity committee's purpose should be to help drive your organization's diverse and inclusive culture. The committee should plan and oversee needs assessments and/or audits and take responsibility for developing a diversity plan based on the findings. The committee would lead diversity and inclusion efforts, report on your organization's culture and environment, lead and be involved in diversity and inclusion events, and be exposed to and involved in recruiting efforts.

Recommendation for Management Involvement Managers should be prepared to communicate plans to their respective departments and to help build commitment.

Keep this in mind as you're setting these goals: You're making 3-, 6-, and 12-month plans.

This needs to happen to improve accountability.

Tracking Diversity Initiatives

Your tracking sheet or system should look like the following:

Goal: _____

_____

_____

_____

Mission: _____

_____

_____

_____

_____

Vision: _____

_____

_____

_____

_____

(Continued)

Guiding Company Value Being Followed: _____

_____
_____
_____
_____

Desired End Result: _____

_____
_____
_____
_____
_____

Roadmap to Achieving Goal: _____

_____
_____
_____
_____
_____
_____

Ways to Measure Success: _____

_____
_____
_____
_____
_____
_____

Continuous Learning Strategies: _____

_____
_____
_____
_____
_____
_____

Do this for every goal you have.

Apply

Once your strategy has been designed, assessed, and arranged, it is time to apply it. This is where the training happens. Diversity and inclusion training should align with corporate strategies and apply to every business unit. Make sure your trainings include opportunities for learning about the following:

- How to have honest and safe dialogue
- How to manage conflict and respect differences
- Overcoming bias in the workplace
- Establishing clearly defined ethical boundaries
- Win-win approaches to problem solving
- Cooperative decision making
- Equity-based justice for all

Ask yourself:

- What message you want to send?
- What media you will use?
- How you will frame the communication program?

Regarding trainers, they could be in-house, external consultants, or a combination of both. Training is going to cost money, but poor training costs the most. That's why you have to go through all the previous steps to know what you're training for.

Assess, Arrange, and Apply That Arrangement

Ask yourself the following as you're evaluating:

- Who will be responsible for managing training?
- What skill-based training do you need that will support your inclusion strategy?
- What does success in skill-based training look like for your organization?
- Who needs to be trained? On what will you base the need to be trained?
- What are your most pressing needs in the organization?

- Where do you begin?
- How will you deliver this training (webinars, in person, online, self-paced)?
- How will you track who attends the trainings?
- How will you track the progress of participants?
- What other factors do you need to consider?

At this stage, the potential for setbacks is high if any of the following exists:

- Failure to get the highest-level leader involved at the beginning
- A general lack of accountability
- Failure to incorporate skill-based inclusion training into the strategy
- Failure to deal with the disadvantages of diversity strategies
- Providing training only because you're reactive
- Misunderstanding what diversity and inclusion means from everyone and not just a select few
- Not addressing the negative attitudes or misunderstandings about diversity
- A focus on shame, blame, and guilt
- Failure to include follow-up strategies
- Failure to hold leadership accountable
- A focus on the business case alone and not the ethical or moral case
- Failure to acknowledge that diversity and inclusion takes time, effort, resources, and commitment
- Failure to help employees see themselves in the diversity strategy
- Failure to make it clear why diversity and inclusion strategies are necessary
- Failure to make it safe for honest dialogue or teach the difference between honest discussions and mean-spirited conversations
- Ignoring the culture—written policies don't run organizations, unwritten rules do
- Failure to remember the inclusion piece of diversity and inclusion

You can't avoid asking yourself these questions. I'm not done, though. I want you all to probe even further and ask yourself these questions:

- What are some of the barriers that are unique to your organization?
- How will you address these issues?
- What do you want to avoid happening in your organization?
- What do you want to be sure does happen?

As you're applying these things, here are some trainings that you can include as you are starting your training program:

- Unconscious bias training
- Communication skills training
- Conflict management training
- Management skills training
- Ethics program training
- Team building training
- Diversity awareness training
- Decision making and inclusive leadership development training
- Stress management training
- Communicating across and managing differences
- Training problem solving with diversity in mind training
- The art of intersectional storytelling

Accountability and Analysis

In this stage, you're being responsible and accountable for the actions you've taken. Here you address what worked and what didn't work. In order to be accountable, there must be clear and specific metrics to evaluate progress. Think of it as a report card and come up with your own grading system. Just like in elementary school, high school, or college, ask yourself what qualifies for an A, B, C, D, and F. Then give yourself a grade based on that.

On the measurement side, regularly reporting your findings in a public forum to your employees also helps to keep you accountable.

For example, you could do this at all-hands meetings, within your company's internal communication channels, or in front of your community partners, and so on. When you do, make sure you bring these things up:

◆ How you measured the organization's success of your unique diversity and inclusion strategies

◆ How you measured leaders on all of the performance indicators, such as: retention, customer satisfaction ratings, productivity and quality, performance ratings, employee satisfaction surveys, leadership satisfaction surveys, or a decrease in employee complaints, harassment issues, or legal actions

◆ What key performance metrics you used, how often your leaders were measured, and how often they will be measured

◆ Who will be doing the measurements of how well your leaders/managers are doing (bottom up and top down)

◆ How you will measure your organization's progress

◆ Whether community partners will have a say in how well they believe your organization is doing in accomplishing the strategy, and if so, when?

◆ Whether you will measure for skill development

◆ At the macro level, how you will attach goals to organizational performance objectives

◆ At the micro level, how you will establish team goals and individual performance

All these set the table for you to always make it a priority. That covers the accountability and analysis piece; now let's go to the final A, Affinity.

Affinity

Affinity is all about sustainability and making sure all your efforts don't go into the "oh, we had a great training that one time" bucket. For many companies and institutions, the single most important catalyst for greater diversity and inclusion is their affinity networks. These groups are usually led by volunteers, who dedicate significant portions of their time to help recruit, develop, and retain members of their network. Affinity groups are a key part of any diversity and inclusion strategy because they are a voice for several identity groups. They help with the development of leaders, marketing campaigns, communications, and visibility. Ultimately, they help boost your employer brand.

A lot of today's problems are caused because people don't understand what's different from them. They don't understand how to deal with changes and so they try to get others to buy into their beliefs. That's the wrong approach. A lot of issues with diversity and inclusion are about deeply held beliefs, values, and assumptions that have been unchallenged, causing many to see nothing wrong with how they see the world.

What we need to do individually is to examine the origin of our beliefs, the reasoning behind them, and the purpose they served. Challenge yourself to be honest, candid, and open about why you believe what you believe. Is there merit to it? I want you all to start with your beliefs because they control basically everything about your behavior. If you are not part of the solution, you are part of the problem. This stuff is hard work. It takes time and commitment, but it's all worth it if you do the work. So I have this question for you: Are you part of your company's problems or their solutions?

Diversity and Inclusion Starts at the Top

Achieving diversity and inclusion in your workplace is a process for creating change through education, collaboration, observation, and intention. Each new level of insight can result in growth and new experiences for individuals and the organization. The work itself can be uncomfortable, messy, and the territory foreign.

Change is easier to implement when it starts at the top. I believe it takes:

Time: The time and commitment to listen to people, the needs of employees, business partners, and clients.

Empathy: Creating an environment that encourages the sharing of ideas and mutual understanding and respect.

Accountability: Developing a system where senior management is held accountable for the development of its employees and the progress of the company's diversity and inclusion goals.

Relationship building: Reaching broader networks and building strong relationships will allow the company to better source, hire, and retain a diverse pool of candidates, which will create innovation and allow your organization to reach broader client markets.

I believe that by training your senior leadership and holding them accountable for diversity and inclusion as a business strategy, your organization will set the foundation needed to create a more diverse environment. Training and developing employees professionally and personally and giving them opportunities to connect with and better understand their colleagues will cultivate a more inclusive culture, which will lead to improved employee retention. Developing a visibly inclusive work culture will be necessary in order to support a diverse workforce, and sourcing diverse candidates requires expanding talent pool networks. The diversity council should be involved in developing and leading diversity and inclusion events, report on your organization culture, and be involved in the recruitment and integration of diverse talent at the company.

Finally, in order to establish your organization as a great place to work for individuals of all backgrounds, your organization should be socially responsible and involved. The company can strengthen its external brand image by having strategic partnerships and supporting early education development programs and being involved in the community. By giving back and contributing to the education of women and individuals from traditionally marginalized groups, your organization will position itself as a socially conscious company and one that values the diversity of its employees, partners, and customers.

The question is, are *you* willing to work through that discomfort in order to achieve healthy, dynamic, and forward-thinking organizations?

In case you're looking for something to act as a guide that you can place in your offices to remind everyone at all levels of your commitment to creating inclusive environments, I present to you the 10 commandments of incorporating diversity and inclusion into your workplace.

Thou Shall Be Culturally Aware: You can't advance if you're not aware of your biases or perceptions of different cultures. Once you understand your biases, you'll be able to overcome them. My recommendation would be to take the Implicit Association Test (Iat): https://Implicit.Harvard.Edu/Implicit/Takeatest.html.

Thou Shall Ask More Questions: Now that you're aware of your biases, let's explore. *Improve* on your cultural competencies by making a commitment to learning about different races, cultures, religions, and backgrounds that are represented by those around you. Ask your coworkers to share with you some of the practices and customs associated with their cultures. *Listen*, make yourself familiar with several diversity-related terms, and explore your curiosity.

Thou Shall Leverage Your Differences: Diversity has to do with the differences around you and now that you have made an effort to understanding them, it's time to leverage them. This is essentially what inclusion is. A good leader is one who is able to create an environment where each and every one of his or her employees feels safe enough to be themselves.

Thou Shall Connect Diversity Initiatives to Your Business Objectives: Devote yourself to the process by understanding how your role is impacted by diversity initiatives and how it aligns with your business objectives. In this complex global world, complex issues inevitably arise, so for your business to succeed, it is imperative that your company is ready to tackle these challenges, whether it is by entering new markets, winning new clients, or managing diverse talent. *Know* the diversity visions and goals of your organization and how they connect to the overall business objectives.

Thou Shall Fully Participate in Employee Engagement Surveys: Fully participating means responding as honestly and openly as possible. It is usually advisable to find an internal champion with whom you can comfortably show your concerns and/or elicit advice to support your efforts. Alternatively, you could hire an external consultant to do an audit of your company and help assess your current diversity initiatives versus your business initiatives.

Thou Shall Involve Yourself in the Diversity Efforts of Your Organizations: You can start by participating in an employee resource group or volunteering to serve or chair on committees that organize diversity-related activities. Consider starting out as a mentor, mentee, or on a team of co-mentors. All these activities will require a time commitment but they prove to be valuable, as they help teams develop personally and professionally.

Thou Shall Understand Your Diversity: Diversity doesn't just come in the form of race, culture, and gender, but also features elements such as socioeconomic background, sexual orientation, education level, geographic location, thought, and a lot more. Everybody has something to bring to the table. What is your contribution?

Thou Shall Be a Paradox: Diversity fosters innovation, which is a direct result of creativity. To tap into this creativity, get comfortable being in positions where opinions differ greatly from yours. You never know what you will get out of it.

Thou Shall Be an Ally: Speak actively on diversity issues that aren't even your own. Any organization will find it hard to ignore the power of the voice created when groups representing different diversity dimensions unify. Also, part of being an ally is making sure you are careful about using offensive and stereotypical remarks. Common social practices that are comfortable for you may not be the same for everyone.

Thou Shall Dedicate Yourself to Continuous Improvement: Be open to learning, accept feedback, and be ready to listen to the concerns of your colleagues. There are opportunities for growth in even the most enlightened individual.

Remember that leveraging diversity isn't a destination. It is a journey—a journey that takes time, patience, and perseverance.

You can download an infographic showing the 10 commandments of incorporating diversity and inclusion into your workplace at www.tayorockson.com.

The Spiderweb of Diversity

You can measure your current diversity level with a quick exercise I call the spiderweb of diversity. The aim for this exercise is to assess the existing company culture and see where there's room for improvement. You want to see what level of cultural competency your organization is operating on. Figure 11.1 shows what you will need.

FIGURE 11.1 The Spiderweb of Diversity.

In the map, you will have the elements of cultural competency. Go through the map evaluating the level you feel is true for you in your organization. The scale should be measured

(Continued)

in such a way that 0 is the lowest score and 10 is the highest. Mark a dot on the scale. Then connect the dots. It'll resemble a spider's web.

Note: You can add, remove, or change the dimensions as you wish.

Now, take a different-color pen and mark on the scale where you think your organization *should* be.

Timing:

- 5 minutes to explain: Evaluate where you are now.
- 7 minutes to do
- 3 minutes to explain: Mark where you think you *should* be.
- 5 minutes to do
- 15-minute discussion: Visible weak spots?
- 5-minute conclusion

Leadership in today's world requires that we go beyond just diversity. Diversity alone isn't enough: Leadership in the twenty-first century requires that we as a society are able to capture the potential that comes from inclusion. With inclusion, organizations can capture a competitive advantage from changing demographics across the workplace and in the marketplace.

Note

1. Juliet Bourke, Stacia Garr, Ardie van Berkel, and Jungle Wong, "Diversity and Inclusion: The Reality Gap." Deloitte United States, www2.deloitte .com/insights/us/en/focus/human-capital-trends/2017/diversity-and-inclusion-at-the-workplace.html.

12

What about Recruiting and Talent Acquisition?

As stated earlier, diversity and inclusion efforts need to be company-wide; recruiters and talent acquisition teams are often at the forefront of this effort. Many times, they get the blame if diversity isn't growing at the rate desired by the leadership team. **Recruiters** are individuals who work to fill job openings in businesses or organizations. Their job requirements typically include reviewing candidates' job experiences, negotiating salaries, and placing candidates in agreeable employment positions. The **talent acquisition team** is responsible for finding, acquiring, assessing, and hiring candidates to fill the roles that are required to meet company goals and fill project requirements. Talent acquisition professionals are usually skilled not only in sourcing tactics, candidate assessment, and compliance and hiring standards, but also in employment branding practices and corporate hiring initiatives. Recruitment is about filling vacancies. Talent acquisition is an ongoing strategy to find specialists, leaders, or future executives for your company.

Retention and recruitment of valuable employees are recognized as two of the most crucial issues faced by companies all around the world. If done well, companies will produce great employee motivation and commitment by creating an environment where all employees feel valued, represented, and included. It also means that retention is higher and companies have to spend fewer resources on training and turnover. Appreciating the employee's varied perspectives and recognizing their uniqueness will ensure an inclusive work environment where awareness of different cultures is promoted.

Sourcing refers to the act of finding a candidate profile you want to follow up on and **employer brand** refers to the process of articulating your company's unique message, voice, and strategy and attracting the right candidates to your company. A positive employer brand communicates that the organization is a good employer and a great place to work, and a negative employer brand communicates that the company will not be a great place to work.

Now that we have all the definitions, let's get into some effective and creative recruiting and employer brand strategies in order to sustain effective workplaces.

Recruiters and members of the talent acquisition team help with developing people in companies. My goal with this chapter is to help companies build an institution that mirrors the world we live in. I spent Chapter 11 discussing how to create an inclusive culture that is sustainable to recruit for diversity. Now, I will focus on different ways to develop effective employer brands and creatively find diverse talent.

Let's start with finding talent.

Talent Search

Stop me when you have heard this before: "The current talent pipeline is broken and isn't diverse enough to hire from." The problem, however, isn't that the pipeline isn't diverse enough; it's that we are not looking enough in the right places. We are not tapping into enough of the world's potential, and it is time we changed that. I want to make the case for a different approach. Companies that are serious about fixing workforce diversity need a strategy that puts the issue front and center and expands the talent pipeline. Companies need to redefine what quality candidates mean in the twenty-first century and address their sourcing problem.

REDEFINE QUALITY
The goal of every company is to hire quality candidates that positively impact the bottom line and simultaneously improve the employer

brand, but I find that a lot of companies look at quality through a narrow lens. No longer should it be defined as *just* Ivy Leaguers with high GPAs. Companies need to widen their scope and tap into the wider talent pool today's world offers.

Austin Belcak, the founder of Cultivated Culture, writes, "Someone who taught themselves to code in a country where technology is slightly outdated will look at a problem from a completely different angle than a Stanford computer science graduate. That's not to say that either individual is right or wrong. Instead, the combination of those two minds tackling the same problem is where the magic happens."

Austin is right. We live in a time when the intersection of digital media and globalization has never been higher. These intersections of markets, customers, ideas, races, religions, and worldviews are shifting and influencing our priorities today and will continue to influence them tomorrow.

Fix the Sourcing Problem

If this is the case, the question then becomes one of how we find this untapped talent and bring those unique experiences and perspectives to the workplace. Sandra Revueltas, my business partner and cofounder of our company UYD Management, suggests that in order to ensure that the magic happens, "we have to diversify the workforce pipeline and rethink the sources." She believes that "it's not about compromising on quality candidates, but about redefining what quality looks like and means. Where are the lost opportunities and hidden gems?"

I couldn't agree more with Sandra. When it comes to the sources that recruiters hire from, their plates aren't diverse enough because they have been tapping into the same sources and expecting different results. We need to move beyond posting job ads and paying agencies to do the work. More effort needs to be made by recruiters and HR professionals.

As Anada Lakra, a former executive in the HR tech world, puts it, "companies should put more effort in recruiting from organizations that provide training and resources to minorities (such as coding bootcamps serving people from underprivileged backgrounds)." Lakra goes on to say that "the problem isn't only on the top of the funnel, but also throughout the recruiting funnel, where many great, diverse candidates may be passed on because they don't meet the 'first impression' criteria in a resume view." Those "first impression" criteria that candidates don't meet is a direct result of unconscious bias and is something that needs to be acknowledged at every level because of its impact on hiring decisions.

Building relationships with minority groups, clubs, international student offices, specialized high schools, and organizations can help counteract unconscious bias in hiring while producing a positive business impact. This approach builds a pipeline of diverse candidates who can change a company's culture from within. The more hiring managers get to know people from different backgrounds, the more exposed they become to different cultures. Exposure helps reduce bias.

As you nurture these relationships with these organizations, you also build a referral network among the candidates, which improves your employer brand because you become known as an environment where people of different backgrounds feel like they have an opportunity to grow. Additionally, building talent pipeline partnerships with such organizations allows you to measure how diversity helps your bottom line. Companies that are intentional about the way they assess their hiring strategies can track data to reveal improvements in metrics such as employee engagement, productivity, and a workforce composition that mirrors the customer population. Lakra explains a solution to the diversity gap concisely: "switching from overreliance on superficial resumes to a more data-driven process will yield better and less biased hiring decisions."

I don't believe as much in the gap in the pipeline that is being reported. I believe the problem we have is the lack of an effective sourcing plan. An effective sourcing plan lays out all the channels you want to use, sets goals and budgets for each, and tracks results so you can see what is working and what needs adjustment.

Beware of Bias in the Recruiting Process

I touched on this briefly in the previous section when I was talking about bias, and now I want to hone in on how unconscious bias affects many hiring decisions today. If you remember what I said about unconscious biases, I referred to them as judgments and behaviors toward others that we're not aware of. If not addressed appropriately, any chance of moving the needle on racial and gender equality in the workplace is shot!

That's right—it's shot.

We can do a great deal of work to access a broader talent pool but if recruiters and hiring managers aren't aware of their biases, then they have not succeeded in developing an effective diversity and inclusion strategy. According to Paradigm, a company that helps organizations become more inclusive, "there are actually four dimensions along which bias can exist in an organizational setting: attracting, hiring, developing, and retaining." It's clear that if we don't address our biases, we don't have a proper foundation to build inclusive organizations and expand opportunities for underrepresented populations in the labor market.

Here are a few ways to manage bias in your organization across these four domains.

Acknowledge Your Bias We all have biases. Studies show that at any given moment, our brains are receiving 11 million pieces of information. We can only consciously process about 40 of those pieces. In order for us to process the remaining millions of pieces of information, we take mental shortcuts by virtue of our subconscious. These mental shortcuts leave us subject to several isms (sexism, racism) and stereotypes. Basically, if you have a brain, you have a bias. It's human nature.

The best way that I have found to identify your unconscious biases is by taking the Implicit Association Test (IAT). IAT measures attitudes and beliefs that people may be unwilling or unable to. After that, companies should invest in other forms of unconscious bias training. You cannot solve a problem if you don't acknowledge it or address the root cause. Anyone involved with hiring, firing, managing, and promoting should go through a series of unconscious bias trainings and there is a whole host of them to choose from.

I recently caught up with workplace culture expert, Vanessa Shaw, founder of Human Side of Tech and producer of Culture Summit. She notes that:

> Unconscious bias training is different than diversity training as it starts with understanding ourselves first. When we become more aware (or shall I say more "conscious") of how we understand others in relation to ourselves—we begin laying down the first bricks of building a bridge towards other people. Don't just stop with the training, though.

Attract Talent Words matter a lot when it comes to writing job descriptions. If you want to increase the diversity of your applicant pool, look at how your job descriptions are written. Research found that using phrases like "driven by" and "results-oriented" have been shown to attract more male applicants. Swapping out "driven by" and using "motivated by" has shown to attract more balanced male/female applicants. Tools like https://textio.com/ make it easy to scan job descriptions for language that deters female applicants and highlights words to show whether word usage promotes a more equally appealing tone for all genders. Vanessa Shaw says, "Remove certain vocabulary from use, such as 'culture fit' and opt for the more inviting term 'culture add.' And always, always avoid industry lingo, excessive acronyms, cuss words, and especially trendy terms like ninja, hacker, or rockstar."

Use Blind Recruitment in Your Hiring Practices Consider trying blind recruitment, the practice of removing personally identifiable information from the resumes of applicants, including their name, gender, age, education, and even sometimes the number of years of experience. One useful tool to check out is Blendoor.

Develop Talent with Structured Evaluations Once you have acknowledged some your biases, it's time to create an environment that doesn't allow you to gravitate toward shortcuts when interviewing and assessing candidates. Interviews have proven over time to be largely inefficient because they tend to be subject to things like confirmation bias and intuition. In fact, a study by Schmidt and Hunter in 1998 found that job interviews can predict only about 14% of the variability in employee performance.[1] Despite this being the case, interviews are still considered to be an essential tool for candidate assessment.

Using structured criteria for decision making leads to more accurate evaluations.[2] Make sure to conduct structured interviews based on hiring criteria that are relevant to the job. Structured processes for recording observations increase accuracy and reduce bias.[3] Structure provides consistency, which enables a fair comparison of fit for a job.

Retain Talent by Creating an Accountability System In order to make sure that managing bias remains an ongoing effort, there has to be an accountability system. Without accountability, outcomes may be compromised because implementation may be lacking. You can create accountability in the following ways. The first is by declaring public diversity goals: Let everyone in your company know the diversity goals you're trying to achieve, then develop metrics you can use to track your progress. Make achieving the goals a company-wide project by tying the metrics to the bonuses of senior leadership and everyone involved in attracting, hiring, developing, and retaining employees. The question we should ask ourselves as we source, screen, and evaluate candidates is "What are our biases?"

Leverage Your Community

What are the current professional groups and subgroups that exist in your community? Which ones can you be a part of? After you answer these questions, get an inventory of the communities and groups your employees are a part of and support them.

As soon as you have done this:

- ◆ Go to events of all the groups you have identified and look for overlaps with your organization.
- ◆ Identify which groups you can sponsor. This is not only an endorsement but it gives you a glimpse into the needs

(Continued)

of the community and how they could tie into your company's needs.

◆ Look for ways to become a speaker to share what your company is up to. This will allow different types of people to be exposed to your work.

◆ Organize events that speak to interests of the communities you are involved in and provide opportunities for members of your organization to be mentors.

Recognizing your biases is the first step in developing practices to compensate for these biases and creating a workplace that supports new perspectives and ways of thinking.

The Power of Employer Branding

Think of your company's employer brand as its reputation and, much like Benjamin Franklin said, "It takes many good deeds to build a good reputation, and only one bad one to lose it."

Take Uber, for example. They developed a negative brand because of the multiple allegations of sexual harassment and a hostile environment. H&M fell into a similar trap when they decided to have a young black boy model a green sweatshirt with the slogan "Coolest Monkey in the Jungle." It was tone deaf and a failure to recognize the negative associations and history that many Europeans have made between black people and monkeys.

The institution of the workplace is beyond the interior—the exterior counts as well. When you have a bad employer brand, you will not be able to connect effectively, much less across cultures.

Here are some ways you can boost your employer brand:

Humanize your company website: Don't be afraid to have your employees and leaders tell the stories of their experiences in the workplace. Allow for a full expression of self, so this can include employees' and employers' testimonials, an explanation of benefits, and so on. Humanizing your company allows your company to focus on relationships.

Create communication channels with the public: Empower your employees to use a multimedia approach when communicating with the public through the company blogs and social media channels. See this as an extended form of communication and engagement with the public. Share day-in-the-life experiences as well and don't get people from different backgrounds just because they are different. That is superficial and people will see right through it. If there is room for improvement in your company when it comes to connecting across cultures, communicate that and discuss the ways you plan on partnering with different types of communities as well as diversifying your talent. Be transparent. Share your values and personal experiences. Create opportunities for online conversations with potential candidates. This type of authenticity and accountability will open up the doors for connection. If people can see that there is room for them to grow in your company, they will want to connect.

Notes

1. F. Schmidt and J. Hunter, "The Validity and Utility of Selection Methods in Personnel Psychology: Practical and Theoretical Implications of 85 Years of Research Findings," *Psychological Bulletin* 124 (1998): 262–274.
2. R. F. Martell and R. A. Guzzo, "The Dynamics of Implicit Theories of Group Performance: When and How Do They Operate?" *Organizational Behavior and Human Decision Processes* 50 (1991): 51–74. doi:10.1016/0749-5978(91)90034-Q.
3. C. C. Bauer and B. B. Baltes, "Reducing the Effects of Gender Stereotypes on Performance Evaluations," *Sex Roles: A Journal of Research*, 47, no. 9–10 (2002): 465–476.

13

Education

The last institution that I will tackle in the perpetuation section is education. A majority of education today places emphasis solely on academics. Who had the highest scores? Who failed and who passed?

I think that's a mistake.

Education shouldn't just be academic. It should also foster emotional, interpersonal, and cognitive development—which means that as institutions, education should create an environment of critical thinking as opposed to indoctrination. How else do we prepare people for the world out there?

Like I said, other than workplaces, we spend most of our lives in an educational institution of some sort. Let's revisit the curricula. I believe that, in addition to traditional academic topics, the following topics should be covered: history, social justice, tolerance, and anti-bias. Let's start off with history.

History

Before I dive in, here are my thoughts on how we have handled history in the form of a poem.

History Doesn't Have to Be a Mystery

History doesn't have to be a mystery.
And yet it is for so many.
I watch as lost stories of identity are trapped in misery.

Efforts to improve representation are silenced
by fragility.

Because to do that means taking accountability
and since no one wants to face culpability, we
teach a watered-down version of history that
doesn't offend the majority.

Marginalized groups are made to think their
origins are from oppression and that they did
so little in terms of contribution.

So the cycle goes on and on, promoting more
ignorance and dehumanization.

Why should I respect you or be curious about
you when all I've seen of your history is in
chains and shackles?

The exports that have made their way to my TV
show you uncivilized and in pregnant bellies.

No I don't need you because my systems have
told me otherwise.

What systems though?

Systems that promote the exaggerated
perspective of the West so it's easy for you to
think of other coasts in jest?

Systems that have hidden the crowns of my
ancestors?

Systems that have justified theft?

Systems that have chosen comfort over courage?

Do better.

History isn't a mystery.

It's a mirror.

A reflection of the past that connects us to
today.

It's a chance to correct mistakes of propaganda
and genocide by filling in the blanks of the
parts of the world that we have brushed aside.

Just because some of us fear what history might
tell us about our current traditions and heritage
doesn't mean we shouldn't tell complete stories
of the past.

History doesn't have to be a mystery so why
make it so?
Doing so is literally dividing our world.
                                    —Tayo Rockson

Recall the examples I brought up at the start of this section, the ones about the person singing the *Lion King* song in front of me and the people at the wedding not understanding the impact of the microaggressions they were uttering. Those come from a lack of understanding of history. A lack of understanding of history does not allow us to learn from our mistakes. Remember our discussion in the Introduction of how our inability to connect has affected us throughout history, in ways such as colonialism, slavery, segregation, apartheid, the Crusades, genocide, nationalism/populism/isolationism, and racism.

When we don't understand history, we perpetuate it. As you can see, history has shown how we as humans have reacted to differences and it has not always been pretty. We have either pushed them away or sought to dominate them. This behavior has been repeated generation after generation across several continents. So why then is most history told from a Western and Eurocentric view. The reason I was met with those microaggressions was because my heritage as an African has for the most part been told from a solely postcolonial point of view. When you do this, you only tell a story of European dominance and you minimize the contributions of other cultures. We miss out on what Henry Ford once said when he was referring to our collective nature: "[i]t is vital to understand human and societal evolution, human responsibility, and global commonalities. When we plant seeds of this understanding in the minds of young people, we plant hope for the collective future of mankind."

The collective future of mankind is at peril when a lot of history books seem to promote sameness and assimilation. That is exactly what happens when precolonial history is not emphasized as much in history lessons. It is a dehumanizing force that not only threatens freedoms but stokes the worst nature of our biases because it doesn't allow us to appreciate the differences that we have had over time.

It's a complicit form of acceptance that there are indeed superior cultures that exist because all the good things and inventions generally seem to come from a select group of people. It promotes **ethnocentrism** or judging other cultures solely based on the values and standards of one's own culture. Not teaching world history in its entirety is a form of telling incomplete stories. Telling incomplete stories of people is a form of institutionalized dehumanization.

Precolonial history should include the study of Africa before Transatlantic Enslavement, the precolonial history of Asia, the history of indigenous Caribbeans, the history of Native Americans, the history of Australian Aboriginal history, the history of native New Zealanders, and the history of indigenous South Americans. This promotes identity because it shines a light on the historical, scientific, cultural, and intellectual contributions of multiple cultures all over the world.

There's a gap in history books, so let's stop widening it.

That being said, let's go into how imperialism, colonialism, and enslavement have shaped the world of connections we live in today.

Imperialism is a state government, practice, or advocacy of extending power and dominion, especially by direct territorial acquisition or by gaining political and economic control of other areas. Because it always involves the use of power, whether military force or some subtler form, imperialism has often been considered morally reprehensible, and the term is frequently employed in international propaganda to denounce and discredit an opponent's foreign policy.

Colonization is the act or process of settling among and establishing control over the indigenous people of an area. It involves appropriating a place or environment for one's own use.

Enslavement is the act of making someone a slave. This usually involves forced migration, suppression, and oppression.

The common denominator of these three concepts is exploitation and the promotion of the idea that there are superior cultures. This has also caused many to have an inferiority complex. I was not immune to this. When I was that 10-year-old skinny Nigerian kid with a thick Nigerian accent in a French-speaking country in an American international school, there were, unfortunately, moments where I felt inferior. I developed an inferiority complex and, for a time, I even found myself wanting to distance myself from my own culture and body type because I was letting Western standards of beauty and culture influence me. This was compounded when my 10-year-old sixth-grade self was approached by a white schoolmate of mine who thought it necessary to ask me why my hair texture was so weird. According to him, the fact that it curled up into balls made me weird, which he said while scrunching up his face like he was disgusted.

What does this say?

It says you're not like me and therefore not on my level.

Add to this the fact that the complexion of my skin was regularly pointed out to me because I was darker than most people around me. Little things like these happen all over the world. Differences are always pointed out, but we don't teach each other how to embrace different backgrounds and ways of life. A lack of focus on this can lead to many people feeling invisible. It wasn't until high school that I learned how to develop a sense a pride in my identity and culture.

It's hard to find a reason to connect if you feel superior to some-one else and it's hard for someone to want to connect to someone else if he/she/they feel inferior. When you undermine whole cul-tures through exclusion, you hurt everyone. A culture that promotes the idea that there are superior and inferior people is dangerous and irresponsible. Cultures that feel superior historically have specialized in gaining power by dividing and conquering. A vivid example of this is the Berlin Conference of 1884–1885 and the Scramble for Africa.

THE BERLIN CONFERENCE

This conference was organized by the first Chancellor of Germany, Otto von Bismarck. The goal of this conference was to determine con-trol of the African continent. The European powers at the time carved up the continent based on natural resources they needed and divided cultures up to form countries that would not have existed otherwise. This destroyed the social infrastructure of countries. Couple this with the fact that Africans were stripped of their traditions and customs, and this ushered in colonialism and making natives feel "less than" in their own environments. This division of Africa without considering tribal, ethnic, and cultural boundaries led to multiple tribal conflicts that still persist to this day. So even though we are no longer in an era of colonialism, the effects of it still live on.

We must acknowledge the weaknesses of our past before we can eliminate them.

Societies have promoted hierarchies and caste systems throughout history and across several generations. Making people subhuman makes it easy to ignore them. Individuals from institutions such as religion, science, and medicine have made up stories to suit these narratives, which have created social structures, social constructs, psychological constructs, behaviors, economic systems, and even biases. Imperialism birthed a lot of today's culture. Separation has been encouraged left and right. If we are taught to view each other as competitors, there is no connection.

History shouldn't be erasing people and killing cultures—it should humanizing people. If we socialize people into thinking that dominant cultures are the best cultures, expectations will continue to be based on this belief. History helps us make sense of the world. The events of the past mold our world today. Just like our choices today will impact the future, so do the actions in the past impact our present. If we don't have a complete understanding of what happened in the past, we will make false assumptions about our present surroundings. Too many origin stories aren't starting with the truth. When false narratives are spread about different cultures or subcultures, we create systemic and societal rifts and therefore perpetuate them.

Social Justice

The idea of teaching social justice in educational institutions is often met with some resistance because sometimes people feel that it is only a liberal agenda and therefore one-sided; but that misses the point. The idea that social justice can only be a liberal agenda is inherently flawed. Social justice education is about teaching fairness, equity, and access. It encourages participation from *all* groups of society and prepares individuals to be change agents while recognizing when other members of the community are being excluded. It promotes critical thinking and an attitude that fights for the values of others, not just one's own. Doesn't that sound like a world that fosters inclusion and connection? We can't hide real-world problems from our youth anymore while refusing to give them tools to look at these problems from multiple points of view.

You see, when social justice is taught in its purest form, it isn't about the educator's personal and political agenda. It is about the encouragement of getting more people to be seen, heard, and understood for who they are. It fuses the concepts of identity, privilege, and power dynamics for a better today and tomorrow. Today, issues surrounding racism, sexism, poverty, classism, access to healthcare, homophobia, Islamophobia, pollution, climate change, assault, and bullying are prevalent in our world, so why hide these truths? Educators are supposed to prepare students for the world, and social justice is a discussion about how people fit into the world today.

Educators should regularly ask the following questions:

◆ What are the current systems of inequality in place and who makes the decisions in these systems?
◆ Who isn't included in these decisions?
◆ In order to implement change, what needs to be done?
◆ How do things intersect in today's society?
◆ What is fair, just, equal, and equitable?
◆ What should the new norm be?

Essentially, educational institutions should promote anti-bias education. According to Teaching Tolerance—an organization whose goal is to help teachers and schools educate children and youth to be active participants in a diverse democracy—anti-bias education is an approach to teaching and learning designed to increase understanding of differences and their value to a respectful and civil society and to actively challenge bias, stereotyping, and all forms of discrimination in schools and communities. It incorporates an inclusive curriculum that reflects diverse experiences and perspectives, instructional methods that advance all students' learning, and strategies to create and sustain safe, inclusive, and respectful learning communities.

Teaching Tolerance believes that anti-bias work should break learning outcomes into four domains: identity, diversity, justice, and action. The following has been reprinted with permission of

Teaching Tolerance (www.tolerance.org), a project of the Southern Poverty Law Center.

The Anti-bias Framework (ABF) is a set of anchor standards and age-appropriate learning outcomes divided into four domains—identity, diversity, justice, and action (IDJA). The standards provide a common language and organizational structure: Teachers can use them to guide curriculum development, and administrators can use them to make schools more just, equitable, and safe. The ABF is leveled for every stage of K–12 education and includes school-based scenarios to show what anti-bias attitudes and behavior may look like in the classroom.

Teaching about IDJA allows educators to engage a range of anti-bias, multicultural and social justice issues. This continuum of engagement is unique among social justice teaching materials, which tend to focus on one of two areas: either reducing prejudice or advocating collective action. Prejudice reduction seeks to minimize conflict and generally focuses on changing the attitudes and behaviors of a dominant group. Collective action challenges inequality directly by raising consciousness and focusing on improving conditions for under-represented groups. The ABF recognizes that, in today's diverse classrooms, students need knowledge and skills related to both prejudice reduction and collective action.

Identity

- Students will develop positive social identities based on their membership in multiple groups in society.
- Students will develop language and historical and cultural knowledge that affirm and accurately describe their membership in multiple identity groups.
- Students will recognize that people's multiple identities interact and create unique and complex individuals.
- Students will express pride, confidence, and healthy self-esteem without denying the value and dignity of other people.

♦ Students will recognize traits of the dominant culture, their home culture, and other cultures and understand how they negotiate their own identity in multiple spaces.

Diversity

♦ Students will express comfort with people who are both similar to and different from them and engage respectfully with all people.
♦ Students will develop language and knowledge to accurately and respectfully describe how people (including themselves) are both similar to and different from each other and others in their identity groups.
♦ Students will respectfully express curiosity about the history and lived experiences of others and will exchange ideas and beliefs in an open-minded way.
♦ Students will respond to diversity by building empathy, respect, understanding, and connection.
♦ Students will examine diversity in social, cultural, political, and historical contexts rather than in ways that are superficial or oversimplified.

Justice

♦ Students will recognize stereotypes and relate to people as individuals rather than representatives of groups.
♦ Students will recognize unfairness on the individual level (e.g., biased speech) and injustice at the institutional or systemic level (e.g., discrimination).
♦ Students will analyze the harmful impact of bias and injustice on the world, historically and today.
♦ Students will recognize that power and privilege influence relationships on interpersonal, intergroup, and institutional levels and consider how they have been affected by those dynamics.
♦ Students will identify figures, groups, events, and a variety of strategies and philosophies relevant to the history of social justice around the world.

Action

- ◆ Students will express empathy when people are excluded or mistreated because of their identities and concern when they themselves experience bias.
- ◆ Students will recognize their own responsibility to stand up to exclusion, prejudice, and injustice.
- ◆ Students will speak up with courage and respect when they or someone else has been hurt or wronged by bias.
- ◆ Students will make principled decisions about when and how to take a stand against bias and injustice in their everyday lives and will do so despite negative peer or group pressure.
- ◆ Students will plan and carry out collective action against bias and injustice in the world and will evaluate what strategies are most effective.

Reprinted with permission of Teaching Tolerance, a project of the Southern Poverty Law Center, www.tolerance.org

Any curriculum that includes social justice cultivates open dialogue, challenges assumptions, discusses hate speech, and promotes cooperation, project-based assignments, and community service. Why not create opportunities for students, parents, and fellow educators to critically think through all the information they are getting? How can you create an environment to foster safe environments? It communicates to everyone that all differences matter. It will also affirm **personhood**, the status or condition of being a person. By so doing, everyone gets to be humanized and identified how they prefer to be identified.

Human societies generally don't invest enough in creating and supporting contexts or institutions in which ordinary people can come together, hear different views, consider the facts, and form opinions that can influence policy.

Are We Going to Pretend That Biases Don't Exist?

Bias is something that we all have. It makes us human and it isn't something that we should be ashamed of.

However, what we must not do is act like it isn't a problem in our society. It informs *every*thing we do and how we humanize people who are different from us. How many schools address real history and feature inclusive storytelling in their curricula? How many offices work together with their employees to include every religious holiday on their calendars? How many families discuss privilege and allyship?

Every time I go to speak or consult at schools, I am shocked by the lack of representation in textbooks. Tell the real stories of colonialism, slavery, genocide, and war. It's not controversy if it's the truth. That's how our world today has been formed.

Don't take the easy way out. That's not being willing to be uncomfortable and accountable.

We can't promote systems that only promote one type of holiday. We can't tell stories that only praise one type of person.

Teach tolerance; otherwise, you foster ignorance.

Teach real history; otherwise, you create revisionist history.

—Tayo Rockson

When dealing with biases on an institutional level, it is important that we start with the same place: ourselves. Self-reflection and accountability is paramount while you create platforms for transparent stories to be shared. Don't be silent about the problems you see at every level. Bring to light the root causes and when trying to look for solutions, be collaborative—get opinions from multiple parts of your institution. Solicit input. This will make everyone feel empowered. The most important thing is to keep going and make sure you don't give up.

14

How Allies Can Use Their Privileges and Limit Othering

A question I get asked often is "Now that I have acknowledged my privilege, how can I help? How can I be an ally?" The answer is to understand the different waves of oppression, as well as limiting othering. **Allies** are people from dominant groups who actively work to tear down oppression, and **oppression** has to do with forces that use power dynamics to limit opportunities and growth for people of different groups by systematically taking away their identities and power.

Sociologist Yiannis Gabriel describes **othering** as the process of casting a group, individual, or object into the role of the "other" and establishing one's own identity through opposition to and, frequently, vilification of this other. According to him, the problems of the twenty-first century come down to othering. And he's right! Othering is the direct opposite of creating a culture of belonging. It promotes tearing other people down and is segregation by design. Even though as humans we have a tendency to categorize people based on their differences, the power to assign meaning to what being different is resides with us. If we engage in othering, we promote alienation and the effects of that. Othering creates disadvantages in institutions. It makes it less likely for people to gain access to opportunities like mentorship and promotions. It also makes people feel devalued.

The fact of the matter is that it is profitable to be divisive. The news cycle—even our sports talk shows—are centered around group-based ideologies. Group-based ideologies become complex because they transcend religion, ethnicity, and politics and include geography, mindsets, and traditions. When you think about this, I can see how overwhelming it is to even attempt to establish connection. It will take a long time to achieve the harmony that I know we can achieve, but I believe it is possible. It might take generations, even, but that shouldn't deter us from doing the work. Just like generations of slavery and colonialism affect us today, who is to say that generations of connecting across cultures won't impact tomorrow? Big-picture thinking is so important.

We live in a world filled with so many people, and yet it is possible to be surrounded by people and still feel alone.

2016 was a particularly emotional year, in which many, including me, felt alone. For context, I had been thinking about the 276 female students who had been kidnapped by the terrorist group Boko Haram on the night of 14–15 April 2014 in the town of Chibok in Borno State, Nigeria. A majority of the schoolgirls still hadn't been rescued, and I was frustrated because I felt like no one was paying attention to the situation. All this was on my mind as I was approaching the C train in New York City on my way back home from work. I just wanted to rest my head, so I found an empty seat and decided to sink into it, close my eyes, and escape for a little while. The only thing was that as I was about to close my eyes, I saw a young gentleman who looked to be about my age wearing a hat with a simple handwritten message that read, "I hope I don't get killed for being black today." I looked at him, the hat, then back at him again. We made eye contact and I couldn't help but nod in quiet agreement.

The brief escape I had planned for myself turned into despair, then anger, then an attitude resembling "I have got to do something about this!" This feeling of not being heard and feeling alone wasn't just happening in my home country with the kidnapped schoolgirls, but also in my current country of residence.

This, unfortunately, is the reality for marginalized people all over the world. As you can imagine, my mind instantly went into all sorts of directions, and I began to think about why the man had that written on his hat by replaying a few events in my head.

A few days earlier, Terence Crutcher, a 40-year-old black man, had been shot and killed by a white police officer in Tulsa, Oklahoma. Months before that, on July 6, 2016, Philando Castile, a 32-year-old black American, was pulled over while driving in Falcon Heights, Minnesota, and killed by a Minnesota police officer in front of his two loved ones. Alton Sterling had been killed the day before on July 5.

Frankly speaking, 2016 sucked, because it seemed like anything could happen when driving while black. There was tension in the air, which even spilled into sports. Colin Kaepernick, an American football player at the time for the National Football League, had had enough and started a silent protest to raise awareness of these issues. This brought about its own set of issues and sparked all sorts of debates.

On one end you could hear things like:

"He must be starving for attention."

"He can't be sincere."

"Wait, doesn't he have white parents?"

"Respect the troops!"

And on the other end, there were sentiments that this was a misdirection from real issues that affect black and brown people today. I definitely agreed with the latter. After listening to all this, all I kept saying to myself was *some are arguing about how Colin should protest instead of trying to solve the problem he was protesting against.*

With all this going on, I started to think about how people of different backgrounds can get involved in solving some of the problems that occur as a result of perpetuation of negative systems today. After all, a large part of the world was finally getting a glimpse of what it is like to live in a world that feels set up to work against you.

If you're reading or listening to this and you feel like you want to do something about this, I want to offer the following.

Understand How History Plays into What Is Going on Today

The number-one thing I always say in response to anyone seeking to be an ally on the issues at play is to read up on privilege and systemic oppression throughout history. There's a difference between knowing the definition of oppression and knowing the effects it has had on education, media, workplaces, the economy, and human psychology. Start off with these books:

- *The Hate U Give* by Angie Thomas
- *The New Jim Crow: Mass Incarceration in the Age of Colorblindness* by Michelle Alexander
- *I Am Malala: The Story of the Girl Who Stood Up for Education and Was Shot by the Taliban* by Malala Yousafzai
- *Americanah* by Chimamanda Ngozi Adichie
- *Long Walk to Freedom* by Nelson Mandela
- *Half the Sky: Turning Oppression into Opportunity for Women Worldwide* by Nicholas D. Kristof

Reading all these books will also give you an understanding of how inequality, inequity, and injustice creates an unfortunate cycle of oppression that in turn leads to many of the problems we experience today. It will also give you an idea of many people's lived experiences other than your own. One cannot fix a problem if one does not understand it. You have to develop a habit of continuously learning of different cultures and history.

Understand the Complexities of Your Identity

Earlier, I talked about how we all have multiple identities. An understanding of your identity against the backdrop of the histories and cultures you're learning about gives you insight into your privileges, how people perceive you, and how you can go into the areas you have access to with your power and fill in the gaps.

An understanding of your complex identity will also help you address your guilt and, sometimes, shame. Make no mistake, if you have committed to being an ally, this is something you will experience, and if you don't address it, it will turn into self-hate. If you hate yourself, you won't be able to love others. When you're paralyzed by self-hate, inaction is the most comfortable action to take. The thing is that it is natural to feel guilt, but that guilt can be a source of connection with people who look like you. I'll give you an example: I often give diversity and inclusion workshops and after my workshops, without fail, a group of white people come up to me to tell me how bad they feel and apologize for things that have been said and done to me. I tell them that it's okay and turn the tables by asking them a question. I ask what they will do about what they heard. Do you know what I hear most of the time?

I hear a variation of these three things:

"What can I do?" "Who wants to hear from me?" And "I am the last person anyone wants to hear from," which I immediately point out as a privileged position to be in.

Don't be trapped by the ancestry of your identity or ashamed of it. Be ashamed of the systems that disempower people based on their identities. When you understand the complexities of your identities and the privilege you have as an ally, you're able to understand who agents of oppression are and identify overt and covert forms of oppression. It is up to you to decide whether you will push through discomfort to do something about what you learn.

Just because history is repeating itself doesn't mean we have to repeat it. In order to work against negative, perpetuated systems, we need allies to please stand up!

- If you're in the media, push for stories to be more diverse. Push past the single-story narrative that exists, as Ngozi Chimamanda Adichie eloquently discusses in her TED Talk.[1]
- If you're in law enforcement, push for accountability and sensitivity training. Encourage superiors and subordinates to spend extensive time in the communities they serve.
- If you're in *any* business, push for diversity to be the foundation of your company. One company doing just that is August; check out their methods at https://medium.com/21st-century-organizational-development/tackling-team-diversity-tactics-lessons-and-data-4e97be328e0f.

◆ If you're a Christian or of any faith-based denomination, encourage integration and find out about other types of churches. Days of worship tend to be very segregated; look for opportunities to practice your faith with people from different demographics.

Understand That Intersectionality Exists

Intersectionality is the theory that the overlap of various social identities, such as race, gender, sexuality, and class, contributes to the specific type of systemic oppression and discrimination experienced by an individual. It is a term that was coined by law professor and social theorist Kimberlé Crenshaw in her 1989 paper "Demarginalizing the Intersection of Race and Sex: A Black Feminist Critique of Antidiscrimination Doctrine, Feminist Theory and Antiracist Politics."[2] Understand that people are not monoliths and avoid using simplistic languages to define groups of people that might share a particular social identity.

So what can you do? Be intentional about understanding different people. Make it your lifelong mission.

Do Something!

In conclusion, there's a lot you can do as an ally. We are in the midst of a new civil rights movement, and I believe that more people can be allies if they want to be. The problem with saying "I'm colorblind" is that it's the wrong response to today's realities. One has to see color in order to appreciate it. The world is made up of a wonderful array of people with different shades, so why be blind to it?

The problem with saying "I have black friends," "I have Asian friends," "I have Muslim friends," or "I have Ibo friends" is that it implies that you're not part of the problem—but, as addressed earlier, there's much work that needs to be done and there is much you can do as an ally. Yes, it's great to have friends in marginalized communities but it's better to dismantle systems that destroy lives of people in marginalized communities.

The problem with saying "All Lives Matter" is that it perpetuates a narrative that persists today that says that since black athletes can make a lot of money and Barack Obama can be president, there isn't a race problem at all. It diminishes the oppressed. Think about it this way: If you fractured your thumb and started paying more attention to it than your other fingers, does that all of a sudden mean that your other fingers don't matter? Nope. So say black lives matter with pride and fight until true equality is achieved.

There's so much work to be done, but I believe we can all get it done if we work together, acknowledge our privileges, and use them to fix the system. It will be *hard* work, it will take *time*, and it will make you *uncomfortable*, but let's not let our *differences* divide us; let's use our *differences* to make a *difference*.

Notes

1. Chimamanda Ngozi Adichie, "The Danger of a Single Story." TEDGlobal 2009, www.ted.com/talks/chimamanda_adichie_the_danger_of_a_ single_story?language=en.

2. Kimberle Crenshaw, "Demarginalizing the Intersection of Race and Sex: A Black Feminist Critique of Antidiscrimination Doctrine, Feminist Theory and Antiracist Politics," *The University of Chicago Legal Forum* 140 (1989): 139–167.

15

Applying LORA to Don't Perpetuate

R emember that **LORA** is my acronym for Listen, Observe, Reflect, and Act, the system I developed as a way to apply every concept I explain; what's shown here is for the Don't Perpetuate framework. As in Chapter 6, what follows is both a summary and an action plan, so take out your journals and make note of all these.

Listen

Listen to the systems around you. What are some of the problematic things you hear being said about people's identities? Make note of them and write out why you believe them to be problematic.

Observe

Observe the agents of oppression around you, moments when people and institutions are othering, the power dynamics around you. How do they contribute to perpetuation of negative narratives? Who are the groups affected by the biases?

Reflect

Reflect on those agents of oppression you observed. Are you one of them? If so, what can you do? What power do you have?

- Reflect on continuous learning. How will you commit to it?
- When pushback happens, and it will, are you willing to deal with the pushback?
- Will you commit to being patient?
- Reflect on the media, literature, and art you consume on a weekly basis. Do they perpetuate negative systems of oppression?
- Reflect on the workplaces you are part of. Are you in a position to create change or call out inequalities, inequities, and injustices?
- Reflect on the education systems you are part of. Are there opportunities to create belonging for different types of people?
- Reflect on the histories and stories of all the groups around you. How will you listen to stories other than yours?

You want to get used to looking at the root of problems in institutions. What is the emotional history behind this situation, group, or issue? How might that history still influence perspectives and outcomes today?

- Reflect on the organizations you support financially. Are they perpetuating negative systems of oppression?
- Reflect on ways you have promoted exclusion and isolation in the past. How will you stop?
- Reflect on the things you share and promote. Are they dangerous?
- Reflect on ways you can be more tolerant and jot them down.
- Reflect on racist languages and how you can stop them.
- Reflect on whether you lie to yourself about the oppression around you.
- Reflect on whether you are passive in moments when you see oppression. Why or why not?
- Reflect on how you can connect to the experiences of the different stories of identities you learn about.
- Reflect on a time you felt different, ostracized, or left out. You can go back as far as your childhood if need be, but recall that experience. How did it feel? Recall this experience every time you find yourself struggling to relate to people's experiences

of exclusion. It won't be the same thing, but if you tap into that experience and imagine it as daily life for oppressed people, you might get an idea.

◆ Reflect on how discrimination and racism can be conscious or unconscious.
◆ Reflect on ways you can democratize access to diverse groups in institutions.

Act

◆ Intervene when you see problematic behaviors that support systems of oppression.
◆ Support artists, politicians, and businesses who promote values that promote a celebration of humanity.
◆ Create platforms for diverse and inclusive stories to be told.
◆ Read at least one book a month about history, identity, race, diversity, equity, and inclusion. The idea is to read about a group of people different from you so that you understand systems.
◆ Educate people in your circle of influence on things you've learned about different identities.
◆ Come up with multiple sources of news.

Part III
Instead, Communicate

16

Actually, Communicate

The single biggest problem in communication is the illusion that it has taken place.

—George Bernard Shaw

After you educate yourself on who you are and on your environment, and make a commitment to refuse to contribute to the negative perpetuations that exist around us, it's time to communicate. Communicating involves elements of both educating and not perpetuating. As you are committing to communicate, you will find yourself at an interesting junction. You'll find yourself seeing things from a more nuanced point of view as opposed to in a binary way. One of our greatest paradoxes is living in a world of nuance governed by binary systems. This leads to needing to deal with several predicaments internally. You might find yourself wrestling with whether you should speak up or not. You might find yourself dealing with fear of criticism because showing up as you are may be such a shock to the norm that it makes people feel uncomfortable. And then you might find yourself not knowing where the line is between freedom of expression and being "politically correct."

Here's the thing, though. As much as you might feel like you're the only one with these thoughts, you're not as alone as you think. Think about how the #MeToo movement started. In 2006, Tarana Burke coined the phrase "Me Too" as a way to raise awareness and create a safe haven for survivors of sexual assault; then in 2017, actress Alyssa Milano, following the heinous revelations that had come out against Harvey Weinstein, asked her Twitter followers to write "me too" if they had ever been sexually harassed or assaulted, and, before you knew it, a movement was spawned.

The #BlackLivesMatter movement is another example. In 2013, three black organizers—Alicia Garza, Patrisse Cullors, and Opal Tometi—decided to respond to Trayvon Martin's murderer, George Zimmerman, by launching a movement that not only raised awareness on the way black and brown people were systematically being killed but also demanded action. In their words, Black Lives Matter is an ideological and political intervention in a world where black lives are systematically and intentionally targeted for demise. It is an affirmation of black folks' humanity, our contributions to this society, and our resilience in the face of deadly oppression.

How did these two movements start?

Acknowledging Ideological Differences

Anger, moments of feeling alone, and the recognition that change needed to take place spurred these movements. The founders were driven by a declaration and a need to be seen as full versions of themselves and, as one more voice was brought to the light, more and more brave people began to share their stories. There was community. There was amplification and there were megaphones. Speaking up matters and it has impact.

Did people misunderstand these movements? Were they misunderstood? Did they inspire hate mail and ignorant comments? Of course they did, but here's the thing: Neither silence nor avoidance is the answer.

Silence Is Not the Answer

We often feel like we just have two options. I'm happy to tell you that you don't have to choose between being honest and being effective. Again, silence or avoidance is not the answer. It's like the late Martin Luther King Jr. once said: "Our lives begin to end the day we become silent about things that matter." Staying silent, when knowing the reality of the world we live in today, is essentially standing up for oppression. Silence becomes equivalent to violence.

Clint Smith, a writer, teacher, and speaker on culture, institutions, and society, once said in his TED Talk "The Danger of Silence," that

> Silence is the residue of fear. It is feeling your flaws gut-wrench guillotine your tongue. It is the air retreating from your chest because it doesn't feel safe in your lungs. Silence is Rwandan genocide. Silence is Katrina. It is what you hear when there aren't enough body bags left. It is the sound after the noose is already tied. It is charring. It is chains. It is privilege. It is pain. There is no time to pick your battles when your battles have already picked you.[1]

So, so powerful.

Most people keep quiet when they know they should be louder, and I want to appeal to anyone that relates to this feeling to be louder than their silence. It is absolutely scary and yes, you will feel alone many times, but the irony is that as you start to speak up for the voiceless, you will be creating connection networks within invisible communities.

The Virus of Apathy

In times of universal deceit, telling the truth is a revolutionary act.
—George Orwell

So far, I've discussed two reasons we need to communicate: one because of ideological differences and the other because too many people walk on eggshells for fear of being uncomfortable. The third reason we need to communicate is the pervasive culture of apathy that exists today. Apathy is described as lack of concern or interest. They say apathy, not hate, is the opposite of love, and it is spreading. I believe that because we are in the information and disinformation age, many people feel inundated with what is going on, so it becomes easier to not care. Your brain chooses what's comfortable for you and then you convince yourself that there's nothing you can do about what's happening in the world because it won't move the needle. You begin to say things like

- ◆ Institutions are going to do what they are going to do anyway, so why bother?
- ◆ My family needs to eat, so why care?
- ◆ It's sad that others live like that but I don't, so I'm not going to focus on that.

Worst of all is "It is what it is." I hear that almost every week, this resignation to the idea that the status quo just is what it is and the only thing that matters is personal advancement.

The problem with this type of thinking is that it spreads quickly. People in your sphere of influence are highly likely to adopt that mindset, and so are people in their sphere of influence. You know who wins in these scenarios? The people who have hate in their heart. The ones who want to promote disconnection and separation based on class, race, gender, gender identity, nationality, sexual orientation, and religion. They count on your apathy because they know it means inaction. Inaction looks like not speaking up for yourself or for others and not communicating despite your discomfort. Inaction makes it easy to recruit people to organizations founded on hate speech and fueled by hate crimes. The people who have hate in their heart appeal to your deepest fears and give you a group of people to hate while promoting short-term wins for you and, as discussed before, your brain likes comfort and safety.

Frankly, apathy leads to lazy ways of thinking because it convinces you that trying doesn't matter. It convinces you that the problem solving and leading will be done by others, so why bother?

William Osler once said, "By far the most dangerous foe we have to fight is apathy—indifference from whatever cause, not from a lack of knowledge, but from carelessness, from absorption in other pursuits, from a contempt bred of self satisfaction."

Everyone's Voice Matters

There is a point. Our voice matters. Here's why I use mine.

I think of my hero, the late Nelson Mandela, who spent 27 years in jail for his cause and inspired me while I was living in a military dictatorship. I think about how hearing about his story and how hearing him say this on TV made me feel:

> I learned that courage was not the absence of fear, but the triumph over it. The brave man is not he who does not feel afraid, but he who conquers that fear.

I am also reminded of the comics I read as a child, particularly *Superman* (as I mentioned before), who is so powerful that he can do almost anything he chooses, yet fights for humanity. Or what about Oprah, my other hero, who was born to an impoverished teenage mother, suffered abuse at the age of 9, and became pregnant at 14 before subsequently losing her child? All this before the age of 21 and now she is the Oprah we know.

I think about all this and I am reminded of some of the questions asked throughout history: "If not us, then who? If not now, then when?" This mindset shift brings me back to my original purpose of creating platforms for people to connect across cultures.

So if you're ever doubting the power of your voice, I want to share two emails with you that I received a couple of years ago.

When I got the message shown in Figure 16.1, I completely burst out into tears. It's not the first email I've received from someone who follows my work, and it's not the last, but something about this email really got me emotional. It took me back to when I was the writer's age and how I was dealing with my identity crisis and looked for inspiration everywhere just so I could feel heard or understood. I wondered what my life would have been like if I didn't have my parents, the late Nelson Mandela, Superman's story, or Oprah.

That *amazing* conference wasn't done with me, though. Figure 16.2 shows another letter I got after delivering my keynote. *Another humbling moment!*

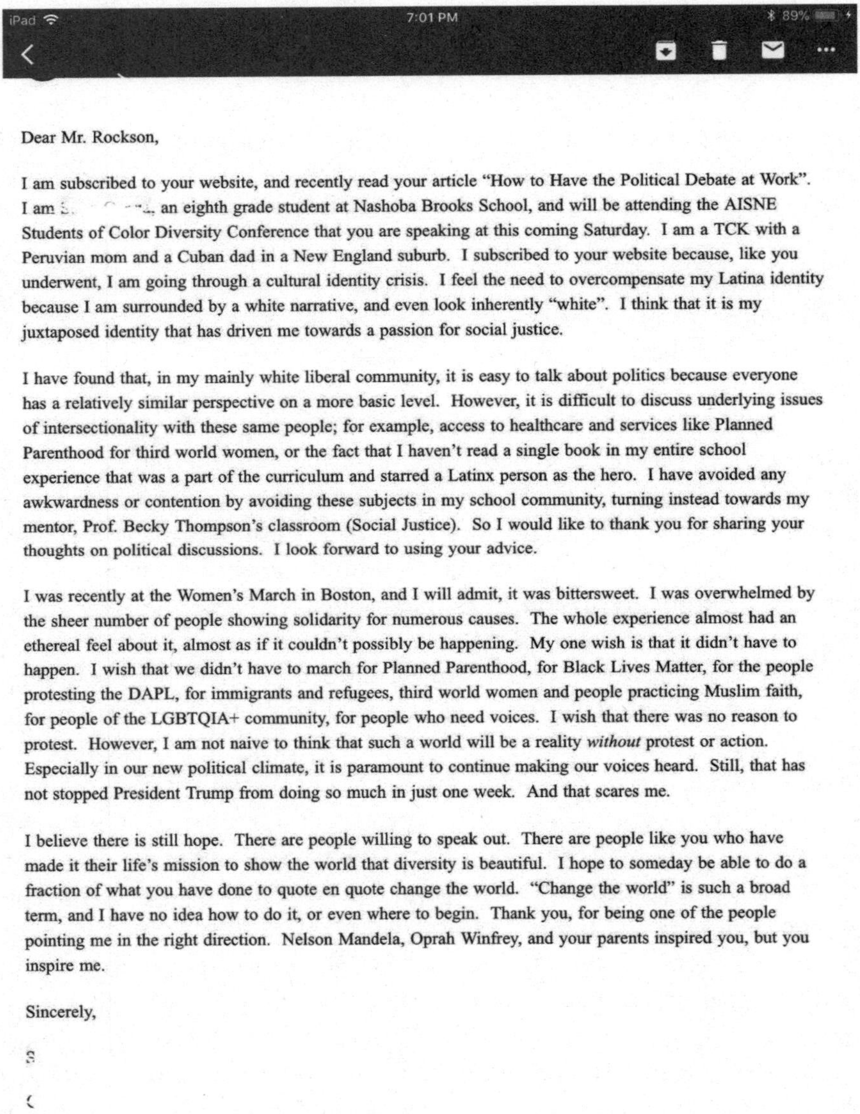

Dear Mr. Rockson,

I am subscribed to your website, and recently read your article "How to Have the Political Debate at Work". I am ⸱ ⸱ ⸱ ⸱ ⸱, an eighth grade student at Nashoba Brooks School, and will be attending the AISNE Students of Color Diversity Conference that you are speaking at this coming Saturday. I am a TCK with a Peruvian mom and a Cuban dad in a New England suburb. I subscribed to your website because, like you underwent, I am going through a cultural identity crisis. I feel the need to overcompensate my Latina identity because I am surrounded by a white narrative, and even look inherently "white". I think that it is my juxtaposed identity that has driven me towards a passion for social justice.

I have found that, in my mainly white liberal community, it is easy to talk about politics because everyone has a relatively similar perspective on a more basic level. However, it is difficult to discuss underlying issues of intersectionality with these same people; for example, access to healthcare and services like Planned Parenthood for third world women, or the fact that I haven't read a single book in my entire school experience that was a part of the curriculum and starred a Latinx person as the hero. I have avoided any awkwardness or contention by avoiding these subjects in my school community, turning instead towards my mentor, Prof. Becky Thompson's classroom (Social Justice). So I would like to thank you for sharing your thoughts on political discussions. I look forward to using your advice.

I was recently at the Women's March in Boston, and I will admit, it was bittersweet. I was overwhelmed by the sheer number of people showing solidarity for numerous causes. The whole experience almost had an ethereal feel about it, almost as if it couldn't possibly be happening. My one wish is that it didn't have to happen. I wish that we didn't have to march for Planned Parenthood, for Black Lives Matter, for the people protesting the DAPL, for immigrants and refugees, third world women and people practicing Muslim faith, for people of the LGBTQIA+ community, for people who need voices. I wish that there was no reason to protest. However, I am not naive to think that such a world will be a reality *without* protest or action. Especially in our new political climate, it is paramount to continue making our voices heard. Still, that has not stopped President Trump from doing so much in just one week. And that scares me.

I believe there is still hope. There are people willing to speak out. There are people like you who have made it their life's mission to show the world that diversity is beautiful. I hope to someday be able to do a fraction of what you have done to quote en quote change the world. "Change the world" is such a broad term, and I have no idea how to do it, or even where to begin. Thank you, for being one of the people pointing me in the right direction. Nelson Mandela, Oprah Winfrey, and your parents inspired you, but you inspire me.

Sincerely,

S

⸱

Figure 16.1   Email from an Audience Member at the AISNE Middle School Diversity Conference.

Hi,

It's me, F⸱ ⸱. Your fan who asked for your autograph earlier today. The reason I did ask for your autograph is because I found your lecture to be inspirational. And that's very uncommon for me.

I don't really listen to lectures. They don't tend to engage me, or catch my attention. However, I could tell that you truly meant and believed in what you were preaching. You managed to draw me, a 13 year old kid doing nothing with his life besides coasting along, into your lesson of success. That's a first!

You inspired me to take action in my own community. I'm planning on starting some sort of diverse club in my own school, where everyone is welcome, but students of color are encouraged to join. I'm not sure what it will be all about yet, but time will tell!

This is a pretty long email. It probably won't be a one time thing, either. You have yourself to blame (or thank?) for inspiring a 7th grader who thought he was going nowhere and doing nothing to take action. Thank you for that!

Sincerely,
The recipent of your first autograph,

FIGURE 16.2   Another Email from an Audience Member at the AISNE Middle School Diversity Conference.

People are always looking to be inspired. Imagine being told that what you say and do don't matter. Imagine living in a world that doesn't have enough heroes for you to identify with. Imagine being told that no matter how hard you try, you will never amount to anything.

Now I want you to understand that that reality exists for more than half of our world today and that we have a responsibility to be louder and braver than all the evil that exists around us. Our voices *do* matter, and you never know who is watching or listening, so don't take for granted the platforms you have and the spheres of influence you operate in right now.

Tupac Shakur once said, "I'm not saying I'm gonna change the world, but I guarantee that I will spark the brain that will change the world." That ability exists for you as well. Our voices collectively and individually matter, so *communicate*!

That being said, I want you to make a pledge that you will no longer accept the status quo. I believe the people who want good things in the world far outweigh the ones who want bad things, so let's use our voices.

Moral Courage

Where's our moral courage?
Its absence hasn't made our heart grow fonder.
And if I'm allowed to speak with candor,
It seems like we'd rather be silent than reliant.
But as we stay silent, we become compliant.

Our indifference causes our code of ethics to
become diluted.
It makes it easier for us to separate ourselves
from real issues. We'd rather be secluded.

The consequence of this is dire because apathy
is worse than hate.
I hope we realize this before it's too late.

You know what to do but you won't do it.
You know what to say but you won't say it.
Common sense isn't common practice.

Where's our moral courage?

—Tayo Rockson

Note

1. Clith Smith "The Danger of Silence." TED@NYC, www.ted.com/talks/
clint_smith_the_danger_of_silence?language=en.

17

No More Binary Thinking

The first thing we have to do as we approach the communicate part of the framework is to rid ourselves of the binary way of thinking, which I notice many systems today promote. You have to choose this or that, and if you choose that, you're an enemy of this. There's no room for nuance, it seems. This puts up invisible walls and barriers before we get to know others.

As discussed previously, we live in a world of nuance governed by binary systems. We promote a culture of debate and division without critical thinking. I am not saying debate isn't good. My friends will tell you that I love debate as much as the next person. What I'm talking about here is when we debate things we don't fully understand. I see this a lot on TV, whether it's sports or politics. A lot of what I see seems to be the promotion of caricatures, generalities, and stereotypes instead of individuality and intersectionality. All you need to say is a trigger word, and boom—all gloves are off. Some people know this and use it to rile people up in order to perpetuate certain narratives, and others feel like they can't say anything because they risk offending others. I fear that we are promoting an us-versus-them narrative instead of an us-with-them narrative. That's why we get into the bad habit of viewing states, countries, cities, and nationalities as having one personality. "Oh, you're from here, so you must be this." "You look like that? There's no way you'll understand this." "That's your religion? Then you must be conservative."

Growing up in two dictatorships, I saw how governments used these types of binary thinking to advance a message or policy to promote propaganda. It's how colonialism and slavery grew—by dividing people into groups and labeling them enemies before even knowing them or giving them a chance to connect. Here's a poem I wrote to verbalize my thoughts on creating more options as we communicate.

Both/And vs. Either/Or

I believe in both and NOT either or
I refuse to believe humanity is this intellectually
poor.
How did we get here?
Where your fear is translated as me not having
a care and leads to despair.
Impulse is to react, react, react.
It's like we've signed a contract that we can't
retract to overact.
Meanwhile, we've lost sight of the many voices
around us.
Voices that can't compete because they aren't
loud enough.
Now THEY think they aren't enough.
But even YOU must admit that being this
invisible is pretty rough.
These days, it seems like we only have two
options,
My way or your way.
It doesn't matter what I say, anyway.
We have created binary systems to govern the
nuance.
Where is the balance?
I'm just as guilty. I'm no innocent.
But as I sit with my thoughts and inspect,
I can start to see the cause of the confusion and
the blurry vision.
The whole picture just isn't being seen and no
one is clean.
We need to examine our lenses and take down
our fences.

If we address our blind spots, we can connect
the dots.
Next time you want to tell a story from your
perspective, be more inventive and think of the
collective.
Next time you ask a question, let it be open
ended instead of close minded.
Step back to look at the whole picture.
You'll see that we are a beautiful and complex
mixture.
Examine the canvas frame by frame
It will be hard, but do it all the same.
Move past homogeneity and create spaces for
more forms of identity.
We all need to apply this sensitivity.
Please don't ignore this because that's how we
got here in the first place where what's limited
now is grace.
Seek to affirm and not to confirm.
Remember, people want to be heard. They
don't want to be a part of your herd.
Life should be liberating and enriching not
selective and elusive.
Your presence should invite other forms of
existence.
I believe in both and NOT either or.

—Tayo Rockson

Each one of us has thoughts, opinions, and values we firmly
believe in. Disagreements are inevitable. This being the case, an
important communication skill to have is knowing how to disagree
respectfully. I am referring to disagreements that lead to discussions
and dialogues as opposed to demoralizing debates. Whether it's an
ideological divide or the courage to speak up that you're dealing
with, knowing how to communicate is key.

That's why I wrote this section. I'll cover ways to engage in meaningful and productive conversations.

18

Finding Mutual Purpose and Shared Meaning

Remember the basketball story I shared at the beginning of this book? The one that saw me, as a Nigerian, mix with my Dutch, American, Cameroonian, and Taiwanese teammates?

Well, our mutual purpose was winning. That was what we were working toward. All our differences and abilities were working together to serve that purpose: winning.

It's the same thing with communication. Whether you are communicating to speak up or you are communicating with someone who has different values from you, your goal should always be to *find mutual purpose and shared meaning.* No matter who we are and how at odds we are, there is something that we all share regardless of the cultures we come from: our desire to be seen, heard, understood, and accepted for who we really are. So how do you get started?

Identify Your Feelings

You can get started by scoping out the issues, examining your motives, and painting the big picture. Whenever you find yourself in a tense situation with someone you don't agree with, look inward and ask yourself the following questions:

- ◆ What do I really want the outcome of this conversation to be?
- ◆ How do I want to comport myself as I have this conversation?

◆ What do I want from the other party in this conversation?
◆ What do I want from the relationship moving forward?

Got it? After all that, ask yourself this:

◆ **How will I behave if I really want these results?**

This ensures that we stay focused on our goals and not on our ego or pride. It returns us to our original intention, which is to have the conversation. Another reason to be this reflective is that it allows you to clear your mind of preconceived notions and resist the urge to blame.

It also allows for you to pause and breathe. Breathing is a chance for you to acknowledge what you're feeling and for you to take control of your emotions instead of being reactive. I always encourage people to acknowledge what they are feeling.

Focus on what you really want from the interaction and how you will behave if you really want to achieve that result. After acknowledging how you're feeling, the next thing you need to do is to make the environment safe. Here are a few ways to do so.

Create a Safe Environment

I find that tensions rise the more unsafe an environment is, and unsafe environments often occur when parties engaging in conversations felt dismissed or unheard. Here are some ways to create safe environments in conversations.

STATE YOUR AGENDA AND IDENTIFY THE GAPS YOU WANT TO FILL

The main reason arguments get heated and become unproductive is because the issue isn't actually being discussed. What then happens is finger-pointing, name-calling, silence, or raised voices; basically, you're getting defensive by being aggressive or passive-aggressive.

Reveal your agenda and continue to state it throughout the conversation. What is the root of the problem you're having and what are the gaps you're hoping to fill in the conversation? Is there something you don't understand that you would like clarified? Is there a behavior that bothers you? Bring it up and say why. Keep the focus on the main thing. You want to ensure that all sides are being clear so that there is no confusion.

Listen and set the table by asking clarifying questions. Say something like "I know that what we are discussing can be triggering for many of us here but just so we are on the same page, I want to make clear what will be discussed and why." That sets the table, and once you have gotten consent from people around the room on the issue and what gaps you hope to fill in the conversation, you can move on. If you ever find yourself or multiple parties deviating from the conversation, a simple statement like "Let's remember what gap we are trying to fill here" should bring you back to your original focus more often than not.

Another way to fill in a gap is to make sure everyone's perspective is heard. Acknowledge everyone in the room, no matter how much you disagree with the perspective. This makes it easy for people to reveal things they normally wouldn't for fear of being judged. It also helps to distinguish between the message and the messenger. There's a popular saying that says, don't kill the messenger. Separate the two. Keep the main thing the main thing. When you do this, you communicate to the parties involved that you don't devalue them as people, essentially that you respect them. People will become even more incensed if they feel disrespected.

As I write this, I am reminded again of the 2016 U.S. elections. It was one of the busiest times for me as a diversity and inclusion consultant because leaders didn't know what to do to manage the dissension that was everywhere.

Let me paint the scene. Donald Trump had just been inaugurated as the 45th president of the United States. On the following day, the world saw a historic amount of men and women participate in the Women's March (over 5 million worldwide and 1 million in DC alone!). If you observed both events, it was clear that the themes of both were the diametric opposites of each other. In other words, the juxtaposition of these events painted an accurate picture of how divided our world is right now—a division that affects not only our personal lives but our professional lives as well. Such was the climate, and the number-one call I kept getting from CEOs was related to how to have the political discussion at work.

The first thing I told them is the same thing I am telling you all. State the agenda and fill in the gaps. I have noticed that in divisive times, most people look to convert other people to their ideology instead of looking to understand the other side. As you can imagine, for someone like me, this is very tough because I am so activism-driven and I want to solve problems.

However, I have found that productive conversations about divisive politics or ideas only move forward when we seek to understand why people think the way they do. Ask questions like "Can you explain to me why you feel like this about this situation?" If it is a contentious subject, try saying something like, "While I don't agree, I'm curious to learn more about what it is you think I am missing." Your chances of converting someone to your side are slim to none, so don't send them articles that confirm your way of thinking. That only creates a back-and-forth that isn't productive for anyone.

Remember, the goal here is not to convert, rather to understand. Acknowledge the disagreement and immediately follow up with a commonality. Something like, "At least we agree on one thing and that is the improvement of our nation/company/family."

The other thing that this promotes is speaking one's truth without demonizing. The key to having an inclusive environment is, like I keep saying, making it safe for all involved. More important, though, is making it safe for *every*one to be themselves. You can't have that environment if your colleagues or family members or students are constantly walking on eggshells censoring themselves. Encourage all parties involved to talk about the issues that are important to them. If you're a team leader, have a meeting with your team and acknowledge the tension that exists. Express to them that you want them to be able to say what's on their mind. The only rule is that they be civil and that no demonizing occurs.

When I go through this exercise with my clients, it is amazing to see the number of walls that come down. A lot of people feel like they would be fired or ostracized if they expressed their opinions. Some feel that they wouldn't be accepted because of their orientations and views. Whenever I do the exercise, it definitely gets heated at multiple times, but the most important thing is that the parties as a whole acknowledge the elephant that has been in the room for a while and state the agenda. These acknowledgments lead to some breakthroughs. Acknowledgment can lead to acceptance if you create an open environment that allows freedom of expression. It's like John Heywood once said, "Rome wasn't built in a day, but they were laying bricks every hour."

Reconcile Paradoxes by Bridging the Gap between Intent and Impact

Another concept to understand while making the environment safe is reconciling paradoxes. This involves questioning conventions and considering perspectives that are unorthodox to us. Some of the foundational concepts in life contradict each other; for example, you need to fail to succeed. The more you learn, the more you realize you don't know anything. Sometimes the things we hate in others are the things we hate in ourselves.

Nothing is more paradoxical in communicating across cultures than the idea of intent versus impact and vice versa. On one end there's the concept of assuming positive impact and the idea that impact is much greater than intent. Let's look at the two concepts.

Assume Positive Intent It was Stephen R. Covey who said that we judge ourselves by our intentions and others by their actions, and it's so true. Have you noticed that we often give ourselves the benefit of the doubt in contentious situations? Seriously, most times we get into arguments or hurt people, our first impulse is to defend ourselves. If we do that for ourselves, why don't we do it for others? You won't be able to see the bigger picture of anything if your immediate response is to assume the worst. I understand how counterintuitive this must sound because of the cynical world that we live in or have been conditioned to live in, but I have found that when you assume positive intent, you prevent yourself from being defensive. It also allows you to take yourself out of the conversation and disagreement to see the big picture. Even if you don't trust someone's intentions, try saying the following things:

- ◆ "Can you help me understand what your intention was when you said that?"
- ◆ "You might not have intended for this to happen, but this is how I feel."
- ◆ "I'd like to talk about what happens when you use that word."

- ◆ "I feel (like this) when you say ... "
- ◆ "I'm sorry that upset you. Tell me how you feel so I can understand you better ... "
- ◆ "My goal isn't to make you feel guilty, angry, or sad, and I certainly don't want any of us to become defensive. What I'd really love is for us to come up with a solution that satisfies us both in our relationship."

These create room for participation and potential reconciliation.

Now let's talk about scenarios when intent doesn't matter as much as impact.

When Intent Doesn't Matter as Much as Impact   If I accidentally step on your toe, does my intent to not hurt you take away the pain you feel at that moment? The answer is no. In many situations, you will find that no matter what your intent is, your actions still have consequences. Your good intentions don't absolve you of consequences. Relying solely on good intent very often focuses on the perpetrator as opposed to the victim, and the victim remains affected.

If you find that your actions are harmful to someone, do more than apologize. Seek to grow and make amends. If the offended party doesn't want to talk to you, don't push more. Accept what has been done and commit to doing better. You might not win the person over, but you will know what not to do next time if you find yourself in a similar situation.

Good intentions don't matter when they promote systemic inequality or discrimination. Say, for example, you're in a school and the only holiday you promote is Christmas because it has been commercialized by many institutions. Your intention of promoting the gift-giving and cheerfulness of Christmas might be well-intentioned, but what you might not realize what you're indirectly saying is that one religion is superior to others—and you validate that by choosing to only celebrate that religion. The same thing can manifest itself in the workplace when dealing with what type of holidays to include in your time-off calendar. If your good intentions systematically give a certain group over another more time off over the long run, then assuming good intentions does little here.

The best way make policies when you're a leader or someone in power communicating is to ask for perspectives on rules and laws you're implementing. You don't want a situation that promotes an unhealthy environment fueled by negative forms of communication, that is, gossip.

I'll give you an example. I was once tasked with the responsibility of helping figure out why there was a communication gap between the Indian office and the American office of a particular company. The American office felt like the Indian office was lazy and did not do things in a timely way, and the Indian office felt like the American office was rude and unreasonable with their demands. This went on and on for a few years so that by the time I was brought on, neither team wanted anything to do with the other. It turns out that on the Indian side, a big part of the implicit culture is respect and it is very common to say yes to requests so that no one feels disappointed, which often leads to deadlines being looser. On the American side, the requests were deadline-specific and so when they weren't received by the deadline, it stoked resentment.

Now, as an outsider, it is easy to see how expectations could have been communicated early on. If leaders of both teams had let the others know about the internal cultures, the toxic environment could have been avoided. Always communicate your intent and the desired impact when making policies, and you will be able to gain clarification from your audience.

The goal to strive for here is getting to a point where your intention is equal to your impact. Get clear about the outcome. State your intention, ask for perspectives, and collaborate based on perspectives heard. Your intention is what you say or do and the impact is what the other person feels, sees, and hears. Unfortunately, many of us today live in a very reactive world that prioritizes a need to be right more than the consequences that come with being right.

Sometimes, focusing only on good intentions completely invalidates the victim's feelings and doesn't make them feel heard or comfortable. It can also be a slap in the face of the victim if their reactions are questioned. Imagine telling someone that they shouldn't be mad for being body-slammed by a cop because they fit the description of someone they were looking for. The victim deserves to be mad, because that's a natural response, and not questioned. It's like the story I brought up in the "Don't Perpetuate" section about not wanting to be "the angry black man" when racial jokes were being made about me. Assuming good intentions sometimes puts the onus on the victims.

If it is a conversation in a workplace or school that doesn't lead to structural and systemic changes, assuming good intent works. If not, it's important to acknowledge the impact and seek to communicate the changes that will be made. If you make a mistake, own up to it. Clarify what you meant, and then ask for ways to adjust next time. It's important to know that it's not about you and how you feel when you make a mistake. It's about how your words and actions affected the other person. Learn from your mistake, and adjust for the future.

How to Bridge the Intent-Impact Gap   If we are ever going to be able to create room for growth, we need to be able to know how to bridge the intent-impact gap. Understand that we judge ourselves by our intentions and others by their actions, so maybe we shouldn't be too quick to respond harshly when we hear something we don't like.

What if we sought to clarify that intention? We all have different ways we see and hear things and have different filters we see the world through. So what if we asked if whether what we heard was what was actually happening. You could say something like, "I'm not sure if you meant this, but I just want to understand, because this is how I interpreted what you said." That creates an opportunity for clarity. It also allows for an opportunity to use feedback to fix a problem and encourage a different behavior instead of tearing people down.

Now the other scenario of the intent-impact gap is releasing our ego and understanding that we should treat people the way *they* want to be treated instead of how *we* want to be treated. Each and every one will find yourself in a position where, regardless of your intention, the impact you cause as a result of your words or actions will cause more damage than intended. What do you do then? You apologize. Own up to it. Clarify what you meant, and then ask for ways to adjust next time.

Don't be too focused on being right or explaining yourself that you refuse to acknowledge how the other person feels. This admittedly is not the easiest thing to do, but that's why it's important to understand intent and impact. It doesn't mean that we excuse immoral behaviors. I'm saying that we can start to recognize that humans can make very poor decisions and whenever we recognize a desire to change, let's use those situations as teachable moments.

Set Your Boundaries

Another way to defuse a potentially toxic situation and limit resistance is to set your boundaries. This is the key keeping your authenticity in a conversation because it reveals aspects of who you are, such as your values and what you care about. All successful relationships require boundaries. Otherwise, assumptions will be made. Assumptions like I thought that you and I saw the things the same way or it is so obvious that that was a joke—*any*one can see that.

When setting boundaries, be specific about what things make you feel comfortable in a conversation; things like tone and body language can and should be brought up here. I know, for example, that when I'm frustrated in a conversation with someone I believe is clearly wrong, I make audible sighs and roll my eyes. A few of my friends I argued with had to point this out to me and I am glad they did, because it allowed me to regulate my behavior and see how my body language affected others.

Setting your boundaries also allows all parties involved to be clear about their needs. When you feel like your needs are being met, you feel safe, so verbalize your needs when communicating.

As you set boundaries, make sure to discuss the consequences for not respecting those boundaries. It just makes things much clearer and it is a symbolic gesture that generates positivity, inspires cooperation, and prevents shutting down.

When setting boundaries, the topic of political correctness and freedom of expression comes up often. Freedom of expression works both ways. Just like you might want to express your opinion without judgment, you should be willing to accept that people are free to react to your thoughts however they feel. All choices have consequences whether we like the results or not.

A lot of my work often gets characterized as me advocating for political correctness, but here's the thing: I don't believe in political correctness. I believe in the respect of ideas and multiple values. I don't think that I am being sensitive. What I am trying to be is sensitive of other people's needs. Consider the use of the following words: *bitch, hoe, nigga, nigger, any* racial slurs, *no homo, that's so gay* or any LGBTQ slurs, and the use of the word *retard*. All these terms are either racist, sexist, or bigoted. It is not politically correct to demand respect. All these words have been and are being used today to refer to people in jest and in moments of tension. They are even being used in derogatory ways when arguments occur. Seek to personify and humanize everyone you meet and if people give you an insight into what they consider offensive and humanizing, respect that. Your words have power, so don't weaponize outdated ones.

I don't support comments that promote bigotry, discrimination, and dehumanization. If that makes me politically correct, then so be it. The thing to understand is that if you're advocating the use of words like these because it's how you interact with your "boys" or "girls," you're basically saying that you want to live a life without accountability. It's rather dismissive if you think about it. Just because things were considered okay in the past doesn't mean we can't grow as a society.

When setting boundaries, don't feel like you can't communicate the things that make you feel human. If you do feel that way, then you're in an unsafe environment. If you're in an unsafe environment, it's more than okay to take yourself out of the conversation.

Writer Son of Baldwin said it best when he said that "we can disagree and still love each other, unless your disagreement is rooted in my oppression and denial of my humanity and right to exist." The fact of the matter is that when you are communicating with people who are different from you, you will almost always certainly say something wrong. If you're being told that you offended someone, don't immediately get defensive. Stop, listen, and hear them out. Set boundaries.

Humanize the people you disagree with. Give them a face. Dehumanization, as I discussed in the "Don't Perpetuate" part, makes us feel better about our ideologies and thoughts. It is what has led to the world's most heinous acts and crimes. That's why enslaved black men and women were once counted as three-fifths of a person in the United States. Always humanize and include humanization in every boundary you set.

ACCEPT THAT THERE ARE MULTIPLE JUST-AS-GOOD ALTERNATIVES

I said earlier that something we all need to do is accept that there are many just-as-good alternatives, because there are multiple ways to get to a correct answer. Think about the multiple ways to you can get to the number 10: 7 + 3, 5 + 5, and 8 + 2 all equal 10.

It's the same thing with communication. Adopting a mindset like this opens up conversations. It's saying you respect that others have a perspective. Ask for stories as well to help see things through another lens. If you want to learn how to communicate across cultures, you need to embrace nuance. Examine your own behaviors, and see whether you are contributing to a culture of black and white instead of gray.

Once you adopt this mindset, you will be able to get into multiple types of conversations. Say to yourself that there are multiple ways to get to a destination and this perspective could be one, so let me listen. It's not our differences that divide us. It's our inability to recognize, accept, and celebrate those differences. Embrace nuance.

Factions

When I look at the world today, I see a
commitment to creating factions.
These factions make it look like we have
limited options.
It's like if we disagree, you have to be my
enemy.
No need to seek clarity or develop empathy.
I mean look around us, so quick to judge each
other based on exaggerated versions of our
biases.
And in the process of doing this, we miss out
on what we are actually spreading. Viruses.

Honestly though, I feel like this is a distraction
from us truly seeing each other.
If many of us can't even quite articulate the
threat that we feel, won't it make sense to
address the raw deal.

The deal is that we are all different so we see
the world differently.
There's no point being tragically myopic in a
world that's already chaotic.
If we contribute to this chaos, the chasms
between us become even wider.

The wider they get, the less human "others"
seem to us.
The less human others seem to us, the easier it
is to choose blinding hate.
Hate that poisons us from within and strips
away our intellectual humility to accept that our
way isn't the only way.

We can't become so attached to despair that
we'd rather choose to become fragments of
ourselves instead of engaging with an
unfamiliar idea.
I say this because we are weakened by our
insistence on singular stories.

Have the courage to examine if your belief
system is based on lies.
Resist the fear of being wrong and backlash by
asking for honest feedback before you speak.
And no, this does not make you weak.
By caving in to this fear, we hurt the ones we
should hold dear.
I know it's scary but rest assured you can still
be brave while you're afraid. In fact, pushing
through your fear is the very essence of bravery.

As factions rise, let's commit to a different plan
of action. One that seeks to work through
differences and allows space for open dialogue.
—Tayo Rockson

19

Receiving Feedback

Receiving feedback is another aspect of communication. Feedback is essentially helpful information or criticism about a prior action or behavior from an individual, communicated to another individual (or a group), who can use that information to adjust and improve current and future actions and behaviors. It is an opportunity to grow and learn. So far, I have discussed several methods to give feedback so now I am going to discuss the best ways to receive feedback, because, let's face it, no one wants to feel like they are the reason someone feels bad, left out, or othered.

If you find that you're in the wrong, here are some things you can consider trying.

Ignore the Impulse to React and Embrace the Pause

When you receive feedback, no matter what your first reaction is, stop. It doesn't matter what it is. Just pause and let the emotion pass so you can collect yourself. Our premier communication tools are our emotions, so it is important to regulate them.

Think of a time when you reacted before reflecting—what was the outcome? What would have been different if you had reflected before reacting?

One more thing to reflect on is to remember what it was like to give someone feedback. We have all been in the position of giving feedback. It might have been to a family member, a mentee, a friend, or someone you worked with. Your intention most likely was to help the person or group. Thinking about it through this lens reduces your likelihood to get defensive and allows you to focus on the message and the impact the message has on the person giving the feedback. This leads me to my next point.

Understand the Intent–Impact Gap

I brought up the two sides of the intent and impact relationship earlier to highlight when assuming positive intent could work and when impact matters much more than intent, so when receiving feedback, step out of yourself and seek to understand this gap.

Ask questions to understand the effect of your action and what you are missing. Understand the true impact of your words, expressions, and body language. Seek to understand how your intentions come across and if there are any patterns you subconsciously find yourself exhibiting.

In the past when I have done this, I have found that in my excitement to express my emotions, I sometimes come across as exuberant and drown out the noise of others in the room. I had to understand how my eagerness came across and it taught me to be more mindful of my surroundings.

The next time you find yourself receiving feedback, make sure you ask questions to break down the feedback so you understand the gap. Sometimes you are just unaware of how you are perceived, so work to bring this awareness to light.

Acknowledge the Feedback

Have you noticed how most people don't actually acknowledge feedback? They might instantly start defending themselves, walk away, or do anything else but acknowledge the feedback. A simple "thank you for letting me know about this; I did not realize the impact of my actions, and I will work to make sure I don't repeat this behavior" will go a long way—trust me. Also, when you apologize, know exactly what you apologizing for. Don't just apologize for apologizing's sake. It will come across as hollow.

> Stop and reflect.
> Don't let your opinions go unchecked.
> Seek to gain an understanding.
> Your mind is worth expanding.
> Look at all sides before drawing a conclusion.
> That's how you get to inclusion.
> What's right isn't always easy and what's right
> won't always feed your ego.
> In order to navigate today's complex world of
> intersectionality,
> we need to get back to critical thinking.
> Just a thought.

I know that many times when we communicate with people who disagree with us, our instinct is to think about what we cannot control, like the other person's reactions. One thing you can control, though, is how you react.

Keep in mind that if people react negatively to you, it's most likely because **they don't believe that you care about their goals in the conversation and/or they don't trust your intentions.**

As a result of this, one or both of you may start acting defensive, passive-aggressive, or aggressive. If this happens, your goal is to remind yourself that the key to having any conversation at all is ensuring that the environment is safe for all parties involved, so here are a few things you can try to defuse any conflict you experience. Take your ego out, make the environment safe, and open up the dialogue. Speaking of opening up dialogue, let's talk about the "yes, and," method.

20
Practice the "Yes, And"

"Yes, and" is a form of improvisation, or improv, which is something that many actors and comedians practice a lot. It is a spontaneous performance without any specific or scripted preparation. The first rule of improv is "yes, and." It is a protocol that allows for anything to happen, and it goes like this: No matter what your fellow actors present to you, instead of negating it, belittling it, or disagreeing with it, your job is to say, "yes, and," or basically accept the scenario as it's presented to you (regardless of where you wanted it to go), add to it, and then volley it back. So it goes back and forth. Back and forth.

"Yes" is the acknowledgment of the receipt of information, not a blind agreement with the information. "And" is the pivot point with which you accept, react to, and otherwise use/build on the idea that has been offered to you.

The key thing to note here is that this does not mean that you're agreeing. Rather, this approach is a device for understanding, creating open dialogue, and engaging in thoughtful, respectful disagreements.

This is how you get started with empathy. Empathy starts with shared values.

Let me illustrate this with an example: There are two people. One loves Cristiano Ronaldo and the other is not a fan.

Person 1: I hate Ronaldo. I think he's too full of himself and he doesn't care about others.

Person 2:   I love that you value compassion and selflessness; I also value compassion and selflessness (this is the *yes*). Here are some instances where Ronaldo showed compassion and selflessness (this is the *and*).

The energy of the conversation shifts from aggressive to conversational. The parties might not end up convincing each other, but the tone is much less adversarial than it could have been.

What this process does is helps you to let go of your own ego, causes you to be more open to other perspectives, and, as a result, you'll have more possibilities.

Less Ego, More Openness, More Possibilities

"Yes, and" is now being taught in schools and workplaces all over the world. It allows all parties involved to become more comfortable with making mistakes and encourages a form of beautiful co-creation that boosts engagement. It also creates spaces for people with different types of learning styles to freely express themselves. I find that although it can be uncomfortable at first to engage in improv, people become less self-conscious because it isn't about who comes up with the best stories but how well a group works together.

Following are some exercises you can try.

One-Word Story

The goal of this exercise is to come up with a cohesive story. This activity is best done in a group of 5 to 10 people sitting in a circle. One person begins with a word and then the next person to the left or right continues with their word. Sometimes, people in the group don't go in a specific order; random people just utter words and go on from there. If you're a beginner, however, I suggest that you start with some level of order and then work your way up to more spontaneity. This activity will improve your focus, storytelling, and your listening skills. It also helps you improve your team-building skills with people you might not necessarily agree with.

Fortunately/Unfortunately

The goal of this exercise is to improve your imagination, critical thinking skills, and verbal and written communication. It gets you used to different options. To play this game in a group, you create a story as a group, alternating between the words unfortunately and fortunately. That's the only rule. The first player starts out the story by saying a simple statement of fact, so, for example:

"On Monday, I decided to drive to New York."

"Unfortunately, as I was driving, I came across a roadblock due to the storm."

"Fortunately, there was a motel nearby that I could wait out the storm in."

"Unfortunately, the motel was filled to capacity."

"Fortunately, the receptionist said I could stay on the couch in the lobby."

And on and on it goes. You can encourage participants to play this game with a theme so you don't go on too many tangents.

A Day in the Life

For this exercise, pick a person you work with or go to school with and ask this person a series of questions about his or her life. Based on this information, you improvise a day in the life of this particular person. This is beneficial for developing your empathy muscles and the ability to look at things from a different perspective.

Improv allows you to learn how to listen without judgment. Your ability to react to changes within a conversation and not be phased will be honed through practice, so don't underestimate exercises like these. Reframe "mistakes" as opportunities to learn.

When you really think about it, engaging in dialogue with someone who has different beliefs or shares different values from you, particularly in a workplace, school environment, or family setting requires you to be able to open a dialogue. The more you are able to expand conversations, the more possibilities appear. The more possibilities appear, the more understanding happens. When communicating, it's not just about you.

Less Ego, More Openness, More Possibilities

Another aspect of communicating is speaking up. Let's look at how to use the architecture of communication model to speak up.

21

Communicating Like
an Architect

In the big picture, architecture is the art and science of creating the framework of our lives. The buildings that we build are either open possibilities or they hinder encounters or connections.

—Bjarke Ingels

Have you ever looked at a skyscraper and wondered what it takes to build such an infrastructure? What about stadiums, churches, and schools? Maybe it is just me, but I often wonder what it takes to bring these buildings to completion. The communication structure that must be in place is complex, varied, and adaptable. It involves the efficient and effective transfer of information, which is what communication is all about. In essence, architects are the perfect example of how to fill the intent-impact gap discussed earlier because whatever is conceptualized in the design stage has to resemble the end product or be very close to it. I enjoy observing architects and studying buildings because throughout human history, our evolution from living in the wild to living in buildings of some sort is a metaphor for what possibilities exist for us when we work together and what barriers we can put up if we don't listen to each other. We can design a world interlocked with connections or one full of barriers.

Architect as a Metaphor for Communication

I am going to describe how an architect brings a project to life and illustrate what we can learn about communication from it. My goal is to use this metaphor to show you how to open up more dialogue. Just as architects reshape our world, so can we!

So how does an architecture project begin? It starts off with three principal characters: the client, the architect, and the contractor.

The client starts it off by setting the expectations, determining the goals, and making sure those expectations are in line with the budget allotted for the project.

The architect must then work with the client to design, draw, and come up with the best solutions given the budget, desires of the client, and scope of the project. This also involves guiding the client and explaining how expectations fit into things like building codes, city codes, and the zoning criteria. For example, approvals from various organizations need to be obtained so that safety is met at all levels in the project. Did you know that mayors have master plans for the city and every building plan has to be submitted to the right authorities to make sure it is in the city's long-term plans for growth and economic opportunities? The same goes for environmental laws: In some cities, there are laws about how deep one can dig and how tall buildings can be. Airport professionals want to know if planes can fly without risk of crashing and environmentalists want to know if birds can fly without hitting the building or if the architectural project is green. Most cities also require architects to post about the project in public platforms and, depending on the feedback received, projects can advance or decline.

As you can see, after the architect meets with the client, a lot of research needs to be involved:

Research on the environment to make sure the structure is safe to build.

Research on the types of materials that would be needed. Some places require that buildings use concrete, some require metals, and others have their own specifications.

Research on the local environment. This involves asking questions, reading, and understanding how the building will affect the ecosystem of the environment.

After the research, the architect then has to think about the logistics based on the information gotten and weigh that with the desires of the client. Think about that experience for a second. Things like the ideal size, number of bathrooms, and color of walls must all be factored in. Imagine the conversations that could happen here.

If, after research, the architect finds out that there needs to be more gender-neutral bathrooms and certain pipes have to be moved, the architect then has to explain to the client that the original plans have to be altered. The potential for conflict increases, of course, but the ability to consider the client's preference in addition to the option you're suggesting requires patience and listening. That's how you push through resistance. It's as much about collaboration as it is about conversation. The conversational nature has to be constant so that everyone is on the same page with design, values, goals, and budget.

After all these have taken place, a contract is written up to reflect all the changes and modifications. This finished contract becomes the contract between the client and contractor. Oh, did I forget to mention that another responsibility for a lot of architects is to negotiate contracts with contractors to hire crews for the buildings?

The contractor plays a crucial role in bringing the concept to life. Contractors are responsible for:

◆ Seeing through jobs like roofing, flooring, and electrical work
◆ Getting the right building permits from the appropriate city and county officials
◆ Managing the construction crews to make sure the project is progressing according to plan and everyone is safe

Now that we have the characters in place, you can see that being an architect is about looking at the micro and macro and then back and forth between them. Zooming in and zooming out; focusing on the people to understand them and then focusing on the external environments to manage the logistics. This is all just the concept stage.

Managing relationships and expectations takes even more precedence in the building stage as timelines are determined. In order to make sure that the client as well as the contractor is happy, the following skills are needed:

◆ Rapport building
◆ Networking
◆ Creativity
◆ The ability to influence
◆ Decision making
◆ Negotiating skills
◆ Research skills
◆ Time management

These skills involve using both the left and right sides of your brain, creative and analytical. If all these aren't done well, architects risk discrimination by design.

Michal Ziso, one of the top architects in the world, says it is human nature to plan and design from human experiences.

The Architecture of Communication Model for Speaking Out

Given the context of what was just discussed, let's dive into what we can learn about communication from architects. The following is what I call the Architecture of Communication (AOC) Model. It involves four elements: Design, Research, Adjust, and Consistently Communicate.

Design: This stage is about designing the big picture of the issue you want to speak up about. Who are the stakeholders? What is the desired outcome? What concerns exist? What are the desires to be fulfilled? Here you are articulating the problem and coming up with a plan for action.

Research: This stage is about asking questions and testing out your hypothesis. Your goal is to figure out just how wide and deep the gap is between the problem and solution. Here you will interview people on all stages in the ecosystem of the problem you want to solve. So, for example, if you want to speak out on lack of representation in the media, you would research media institutions, people who put out stories in the media, and the people who are underrepresented. You are going to find out what people want, why the solution isn't happening sooner, who the influencers are in your potential solution, what behaviors need to change, which institutions you need to include, and what will make your solution sustainable.

Adjust: Adjusting is about making changes to your design. How can you make it more inclusive and impactful? You'll be using the new information to redesign. This can also be a collaborative step, because your plan will include activating influencers who are close to the problem and sometimes institutions that can do something about it. It's the redesign after you check back in with stakeholders. You're co-creating and designing relationships that work for you as well as deciding what your messaging will be and which platform it will be on.

Consistently communicate: Like an architect, you constantly show up and communicate your message through all the channels and are transparent. You'll have good days and bad days, but pushing through is what will get your message heard.

Curiosity Opens the World

If you're only focused on being right, you won't
release your ego.
If you release your ego, you'll ask questions.
If you'll ask questions, you'll open your mind.
If you open your mind, you'll appreciate
difference.
If you appreciate difference, you'll understand
the other side of privilege.
If you understand the other side of privilege,
you'll strive for equity.
We live in a world that our curiosity has formed.
The question is, are you curious enough?

—Tayo Rockson

22

What Nelson Mandela Taught Us about Seeing the Bigger Picture

The late great Nelson Mandela, my hero, died on December 5, 2013 at the age of 95. One of the remarkable things about him was that by the time he emerged from prison at the age of 71, he had spent 38% of his life in jail. *Twenty-seven years*! But it was what he did with the remaining 24 years of his life that would change the world forever. He used the remaining 24 years of his life to teach the world how to see the bigger picture.

Affectionately known as Madiba, which means father, he certainly served as a father figure for many across the globe. I have spent countless hours studying his leadership style, and his ability to see the bigger picture was, in my opinion, his greatest strength as a global leader. It is what made him a great communicator. Here are some examples of Mandela's understanding the bigger picture.

Mandela Found Freedom in Forgiveness

For many people, being imprisoned for 27 years would plant seeds of bitterness and vengeance, but Nelson Mandela chose to see the bigger picture upon his release. Here's what he said after being released:

As I walked out the door toward the gate that would lead to my freedom, I knew if I didn't leave my bitterness and hatred behind, I'd still be in prison.

—Nelson Mandela

He showed the world what true forgiveness was like by fully forgiving his opponents, even though he was now in a position of power over them. In the four years from when he left prison in 1990 to when he was elected the first black South African president, Mandela used his time to bring parties from different ethnic groups together. He created environments for open discussion among groups that had fought each other for years because he realized that the bigger picture was unity, and that if South Africa was ever going to be great, everyone needed to have a seat at the table.

This was evident in how he played a big role in the Truth and Reconciliation Commission, which was formed by the new South African government in 1995. Its goal was to help heal the country and bring about a reconciliation of its people by uncovering the truth about human rights violations that had occurred during the period of apartheid. Its emphasis was on gathering evidence and uncovering information—from both victims and perpetrators—and not on prosecuting individuals for past crimes, which is how the commission's focus differed from the Nuremberg trials that prosecuted Nazis after World War II. Mandela helped bring together whites and blacks to help shape a better tomorrow. This is something we can all learn from. Don't run away from what you don't understand; rather, seek to give everyone a voice and work out a solution from there.

One could say that, in a way, Mandela's 27 years in prison saved him. It gave him time to develop his communication style as well as a new perspective. He became someone with a willingness to open his heart, mind, and soul to the problems that existed around him. He allowed himself to develop a space for change and therefore better understanding.

One of the most difficult things is not to change society but to change yourself.

—Nelson Mandela

He was flexible. Nelson Mandela went from being the personification of opposition to being a symbol of freedom, and he was able to do this because of his ability to be flexible and shift his communication style. Mandela recognized that he needed to change his style in order to do what was best for his country.

That's something a culturally aware leader has to be aware of today. Whether it's learning how to use social media tools or shifting a rigid mindset you might have previously held in order to pave the way for cooperation, you have to be open to the idea of change. When I say change I don't mean changing who you are completely and standing for nothing but rather changing your approach in solving a problem. Mandela wanted a South Africa where black people had a voice before he went to prison and he wanted the same thing when he came out, but he was less militant about it. A change in approach, not a change in values. Flexibility.

Mandela Was Focused on Goals and a Mission beyond Himself

Even before Mandela went to prison, he had a deep sense of purpose that was not about him. Here's what he said in his speech at the opening of his trial for sabotage in Pretoria on April 20, 1964:

> During my lifetime I have dedicated myself to this struggle of the African people. I have fought against white domination, and I have fought against black domination. I have cherished the ideal of a democratic and free society in which all persons live together in harmony and with equal opportunities. It is an ideal which I hope to live for and to achieve. But if need be, it is an ideal for which I am prepared to die.[1]

This was something he continued to live by every day until his death. For him, the big picture was ensuring that true equality existed. His ability to understand his role in the grand scheme of things was remarkable. It didn't matter what happened to him as long as his fellow countrymen and -women got to experience better lives. He wanted to ensure that the next generation did not experience the hardships his generation went through and so he continued to fight.

Surround Yourself with People Drastically Different from You

This is really important because this gives you insight into the lives of people from other cultures. You can see this when Nelson Mandela first got out of prison. The regime and bodies of government he formed were a mix of people from different races, beliefs, and former oppressors. He even invited one of his former white wardens to his inauguration as president. Mandela understood that having different perspectives in his cabinet would give him a well-rounded outlook and make him more open-minded to solving South Africa's problems. Sharing power allowed him to overcome his personal prejudices, which led him to winning a Nobel Peace Prize that he—wait for it—shared with the white president who preceded him, F. W. de Klerk.

Mandela Knew How to Find Unity in Global Moments

Part of being a great communicator is recognizing opportunities, and Nelson Mandela did this often. Perhaps the most famous example of this was during the 1995 Rugby World Cup final, when South Africa was playing against New Zealand. Up until that point, rugby in South Africa was a direct symbol of apartheid. It was a primarily white sport and many black South Africans actively rooted against the team. However, Mandela saw things differently. To him, he saw the moment as an opportunity to bring the nation together. His advisors disagreed strongly, but he walked on to that stage where millions all over the world saw him draped in the Springbok jersey, which had been the symbol of hatred for so many, and South Africans of all races chanted: Nelson! Nelson! Nelson!

Author John Carlin said, "It was far, far, far more than a sporting event. I've never come across a more politically significant, emotional ... moment than what was witnessed at the World Cup."

Educate Yourself

When he was in prison, Mandela learned Afrikaans, the language of the dominant white, so that he could communicate with his wardens as well as white South Africans in general.

A culturally aware leader is aware that there are many moving parts in the world and that there is no *one* way to communicate, so he or she puts in the time to learn nuances, behaviors, and norms of other cultures. Some ways to do this as a culturally aware leader are to pick up new languages and travel. Travel is one of those things that you can't go to school for. You can't learn it in theory. You can only learn it in practice. You might not have the money to go to other countries, but you can start by visiting a different city, state, or municipality for a weekend and talk to locals. You're going to be learning something new and adding it to your repertoire. You'll also improve your cultural sensitivity.

As for learning languages, there are many platforms: Duolingo, Livemocha, Busuu. The great thing about using some of these apps is that it lets you connect with other fellow language learners in different parts of the world, learn about them, and vice versa.

Once people from other cultures and backgrounds see that you're making an effort, they will be more helpful to you, and this leads to collaborative efforts.

> *Education is the most powerful weapon which you can use to change the world.*
>
> —Nelson Mandela

Today's world is more diverse and digital than it has ever been; that's amazing, because it means that we have the potential to connect more with others, as well as become more aware about the world and all the cultures in it. This diversity fosters innovation; it brings about fresh, interesting perspectives. Last but not least, it helps in crisis management. In order to be better global leaders in the twenty-first century, one has to know how to communicate across cultures digitally and physically. All this starts with being humble enough to see the big picture, something Nelson Mandela personified.

He knew that the global environment is an ever-changing place and that in order to lead and communicate in the global mosaic, he put in the work to understand his fellow citizens and neighbors. He did not think that one culture was better than any other. Thinking this way is a lot easier said than done. Trust me, I know. I was constantly moving between countries and continents as the son of a diplomat myself, but the more comfortable I got with being comfortable and accepting my ignorance, the more open-minded I became and the more relatable I was to other people and other cultures.

December 5 is a day I will never forget. Even though Mandela died a few years ago, his spirit lives on today. Let us learn how to see the bigger picture in our global world. Our world today has shown us that a lot of work still needs to be done to give everyone a voice, but let Nelson Mandela be a reminder to you all that unity is possible and that we can all truly use our differences to make a difference.

Note

1. "I Am Prepared to Die," press release, Nelson Mandela Foundation, 20 April 2011, www.nelsonmandela.org/news/entry/i-am-prepared-to-die.

23

The Path to Reconciliation in Rwanda After Genocide

From April 7, 1994 to July 1994, a 100-day period, members of the Hutu majority government conducted a genocidal attack against members of the Tutsi tribe. The catalyst for this attack is said to have been the April 6, 1994, shooting down of an airplane carrying the Rwandan president at the time, Juvénal Habyarimana, as well as the Hutu president of Burundi, Cyprien Ntaryamira. Everyone on board was killed and the Tutsi were blamed for this attack.

Members of the Rwandan army, who were mostly Hutus, passed out clubs and machetes to fellow Hutu civilians to execute Tutsis on sight. If they showed mercy, they could potentially be arrested for being collaborators. This turned into despicable mass killings. Many instances saw men killing wives and churches becoming places for mass murders. Members of the clergy would sometimes arrange for people to attend churches, where they would subsequently be executed. By the time it was all said and done, nearly a million people had been killed, most of them Tutsis, based on their ethnicity. That's about 1 in 5 Rwandans. Reportedly, 100,000 Hutus were also killed, some of them as a result of revenge killings by the Tutsis and some by Hutu extremists. The genocide reportedly ended after Tutsi rebels overtook the government.[1]

Why the hate, though?

How did it get to the point where your affiliation to an ethnic group led to your death? What caused the ethnic divide? A lot of it can be traced back to colonialism. Germany initially colonized present-day Rwanda and Burundi in the late nineteenth century, and with their colonization, they instituted a feudal system, which is a system of land ownership and duties. You could ascend from one group to another based on your economic situation. In the system, the Tutsi minority usually ended up on top. After World War I, the League of Nations (the precursor to the United Nations) basically gave Rwanda and Burundi to Belgium.

Belgium instituted policies that forced citizens of Rwanda and Burundi to carry cards that displayed their ethnicity. French became the common language and Christianity became the national religion. There were approximately 80% Hutus, 19% Tutsis, and 1% Twa.[2] Despite this majority status, Hutus were still seen as inferior to the colonizers. They were refused access to higher education, politics, and administrative jobs. The system was a form of apartheid, which was also practiced in South Africa. There is some dispute about how the Hutus and Tutsis were differentiated. Belgians were said to have differentiated between them by height, nose size, skin color, and eye type. Tutsis were said to have a more European look because of their light skin, height, thin nose, and lips. Hutus, on the other hand, have darker skin and shorter builds.[3] However, many Rwandans don't believe that there are distinguishable physical characteristics between the two groups.

Regardless of this, there is one thing that cannot be denied, and that is that this division based on ethnic groups was a direct result of colonization. During colonization, "Hutus" were people who farmed crops, while "Tutsis" were people who tended livestock. These differences in class became differences in ethnic groups.

Classic divide and rule, instituted by both the Germans and Belgians.

Such was the climate during the genocide. After decades of programmed hate and division, the assassination of the Hutu president made it easy to spread propaganda messages of hate that the Tutsis were coming after the Hutus.

How would Rwanda recover post-genocide?

How would reconstruction and reconciliation work in such a climate?

How would survivors come face to face with perpetrators?

What about the pain, trauma, hatred, the quest for revenge, forgiveness?

How would all these work?

As you can imagine, the implications on a political, legal, economical, and cultural level were monumental.

Reconciliation started with seeking justice through the International Criminal Tribunal for Rwanda, local courts, and national courts. Opportunities were provided for reconciliation and healing as victims of the genocide were granted the chance to learn the truth about what had happened to their loved ones and families, while perpetrators had the chance to confess to their crimes, ask for forgiveness, and show remorse. Many perpetrators also had to work for forgiveness by building houses for survivors. This must have been an incredibly difficult process, and I cannot even imagine what it felt like to come face to face with the people who had murdered your loved ones. I get chills just thinking about it, but there was no sweeping the issues under the rug. There was no denying the magnitude of the effects. Some people forgave and some didn't, but the opportunity was presented.

According to Search for Common Ground, which is an organization that partners with people around the world to ignite shared solutions to destructive conflicts by working at all levels of society to build sustainable peace through three main avenues (dialogue, media, and community), Rwanda has made great strides post-genocide. It has seen impressive economic growth and a concerted effort from national and international actors to heal wounds and rebuild communities. This process is hailed as a modern-day success story in post-genocide reconciliation and development.[4]

It certainly hasn't been perfect, though, as Rwanda is ruled by an authoritarian government headed by President Paul Kagame, who has been the president since 2000. He has been criticized in the past for his human rights record and state-sponsored media and style of governance. That being said, Kagame came into power with two main goals: to unify people and to reduce poverty, and there have been efforts made to achieve these goals. I already discussed the efforts to reconcile. For the economic part, Kagame created an advisory team that sought advice from emerging nations like China, Thailand, and Singapore. It was part of his national program, called Vision 2020, whose intention is to make Rwanda a middle-income country by 2020. It included clear, specific goals that could be quantified, including reconstruction, infrastructure, and improving multiple sectors of the government and economy. As of the time of writing this book, it does not quite look like Rwanda will be a middle-economy country by 2020,[5] but it has a gender-balanced cabinet with 50% of its members women, met over half of the goals it set out to achieve in the Vision 2020 plan,[6] and has gone from being one of 10 poorest nations in the world to one of the fastest-growing economies.

There is still a lot of work to be done, but what I hope this case study shows is the importance of reconciliation and creating a path for healing.

Notes

1. Zack Beauchamp, "Rwandan's Genocide—What Happened, Why It Happened, and Why It Still Matters," Vox, 10 April 2014, www.vox.com /2014/4/10/5590646/rwandan-genocide-anniversary.

2. "Rwanda." *Worldmark Encyclopedia of Nations*, 2007, Encyclopedia.com, www.encyclopedia.com/places/africa/rwandan-political-geography /rwanda - 3426900151.

3. Kimberly Fornace, "The Rwandan Genocide," *Beyond Intractability*, April 2009, www.beyondintractability.org/casestudy/fornace-rwandan.

4. https://www.sfcg.org/wp-content/uploads/2018/07/SFCG_Rwanda_ Country_Strategy_2017-2021.pdf.

5. David Himbara, "Kagame, Inform Rwandans Vision 2020 Is Dead," *The Rwandan*, 5 July 2018, www.therwandan.com/kagame-inform-rwandans-vision-2020-is-dead/.

6. Gregory Warner, "It's The No. 1 Country For Women In Politics—But Not In Daily Life," NPR, 29 July 2016, www.npr.org/sections/goatsandsoda/ 2016/07/29/487360094/invisibilia-no-one-thought-this-all-womans-debate-team-could-crush-it.

24

Healing Our World Today

We are defined by the choices we make and, throughout history, we have given in to our desire for more power at the expense of building connections. Systems and cultures have been built on this bad habit, which has created a cycle that we can't seem to shake. We all come from similar roots as *Homo sapiens*. Throughout history, as humans have migrated, we have formed our own cultures relative to our geography and personal experiences. We came up with a supposed natural order of things and invented different ways to categorize people based on several hierarchical methods.

Despite many of us knowing this deep down and understanding that the world isn't divided into binaries, we have resorted to trying to eliminate people who are different from us, people who have different ideas from us, and people who look different from us. The result has been a hurting world that lacks tolerance and compassion—a world that moves on too quickly from its crimes and does not work through grievances. There's barely any acknowledgment, reconciliation, or any form of atonement.

Avoiding Cancel Culture

In the past, we dismissed people and institutionalized doing so as law and unwritten laws. Today, I fear that we are making dismissing people the cool thing to do with "cancel culture." **Cancel culture** is a term used to refer to the phenomenon of "canceling," or no longer morally, financially, and/or digitally supporting people—usually celebrities—or things that many have deemed unacceptable or problematic.

We are canceling people before we even get to know them. I'm noticing a deeper trend across the world to just cancel things and people we don't agree with, but here's the thing: As Michael Eric Dyson once said, "digital culture cannot deal with analog realities." In an analog reality, people make mistakes because we are all, well, human, and we are multifaceted. I want us to be able to call people, brands, and things out while creating a path for redemption. Liz Kleinrock, an anti-bias educator and the 2018 Teaching Tolerance Award winner, says the following:

> Social media provides us the luxury of picking and choosing who we listen to, and tuning out when we don't feel like engaging. Conversations around equity are uncomfortable and challenging, and when times are tough, many of us revert back to what's familiar and easy. This might be challenging yourself to confront your privilege, "call in" a friend or coworker who made a questionable comment, or look for the humanity in someone who you assume you could never relate to.
>
> I've been worrying more and more that the more we demand perfection from each other (despite reminding our students the importance of making and learning from mistakes), the more often we write each other off before seeking to understand. Of course racism, homophobia, xenophobia, religious intolerance, etc. are wrong. But instead of being angry at where people are at on the spectrum of equity, try questioning WHY they're at that particular point on the spectrum.
>
> Again, humans are systems that need to be dismantled as much as the oppressive systems we're living in. We're not going to see the end of racism or discrimination in our lifetime, and that's a hard pill to swallow. But if you start with yourself, your students, or your children, these steps WILL make a difference ... We cannot hope to fix problems in our communities if we do not talk about them.[1]

Some of us don't talk to each other enough, and when we do talk, we very often attack until we erase. If we continue promoting this type of culture, we will pass negative habits onto the next generation. Like Peggy O'Mara once said, "the way we talk to our children becomes their inner voice."

We All Need to Be Forgiven

I once heard Wayne Dyer talk about how the Babemba tribe of southern Africa, namely Zambia and the Congo, approach forgiveness, and I think we can apply some of that approach to today's world.

It is said that when someone misbehaves or acts irresponsibly he/she/they are placed in the center of the village. A community then gathers around the accused person to hear each person in the community of every age tell the accused all the good things the one in the center ever did in his/her/their lifetimes.

Every experience is recounted including the positive characteristics, attributes, and strengths is brought up and discussed.

What if we not only pointed out the negative aspects of people but also reminded people of their humanities?[2]

Now I am not saying all this to excuse immoral behaviors. Things like sexual assault, murder, and crimes against humanity should continue to be acknowledged and brought to light, and should receive actual punishment. What I am saying is that I do not want us to promote systems that promote harm and hate and perpetuate ignorance without any form of accountability or growth.

I do fear that we are missing out on nuance when we criticize people without creating a path for redemption. What are we telling our world if we can't make mistakes or have difficult conversations? It's like you're saying that there is very little opportunity to be able to learn from past mistakes. This leads to no engagement.

Open dialogue needs to be met with open-mindedness. We all make mistakes. What matters is that we learn from them and how we can improve, repent, or work toward not repeating them.

Open Dialogue and Open-Mindedness

If we don't create a culture of forgiveness and open dialogue, how are we going to move forward? I do worry about how many of us are impeding progress if we choose to lead with pitchforks first. Now don't get me wrong—wrongdoings need to be called out, but connecting across cultures is so much more nuanced than we pretend it is. It involves work. It involves discomfort and mistakes. That's inevitable when you talk to people who are different from you.

At the same time, while we are creating a culture of open dialogue, we need a culture of open-mindedness. Just because we don't understand something doesn't mean we shouldn't see it or acknowledge it. We need to let go of thinking that our way is law; that's arrogant and ego-driven.

If the past few years are any indication of our future, we can recognize that there's opportunity to do better about systemic problems we have normalized. Let's also not forget that a lot of those normalized things have included many of us as perpetrators. As perpetrators and changemakers alike, we have to simultaneously be willing to be brave enough to let go of bad behaviors that have made us comfortable in the past and humble enough to accept allies who are willing to change. That's how we progress.

At the end of the day, we are all we have, and we are complex. Just because we don't agree with each other doesn't mean we should be quick to dismiss. While we are at it, we need to be careful not to engage in oppression Olympics. **Oppression Olympics** is a term used when two or more groups compete or engage in conversations to prove that their marginalized group is more oppressed than the other.

When we start comparing ourselves with each other about who has had it worse, we miss out on the bigger picture, which leads to an environment of animosity without listening because no interests are actually being met.

Notes

1. Teachandtransform, "Liz Kleinrock on Instagram: '@Tayorockson and I Have Had Ongoing Conversation All Week about "Cancel Culture" and the Role That Forgiveness Plays in Achieving Justice...," Instagram, www.instagram.com/p/Bt9A0dfB_jV/.
2. http://youtu.be/UuP0KDmneiE.

25

The Importance of Cultural Awareness

Cultural awareness is the recognition of our cultural traits, such as language, beliefs, art, music, values, history, and perception. This knowledge, when acquired, becomes the foundation of our communication with others, especially those of different backgrounds, because it gives us an entirely fresh perspective and the drive to learn more about them.

The first stage of cultural awareness involves digging deeper into our identities to derive more meaning about the things we may not know or understand. This level of knowledge forms the basis for the next stage of this awareness, which is understanding other cultures around us.

As we begin to investigate and interact with people from different cultures, we inevitably come across routines and behaviors that are quite different from how we do things. Sometimes, these behaviors might even seem absurd to us. When we begin to notice these differences, the best thing is to acknowledge, accept, and appreciate them.

Problems usually arise when we are too rigid and leave no room for flexibility. Our lifestyles, beliefs, religions, experiences, and values are often things passed down from our ancestors and families, and these are the things that make us unique and distinguish us from those of other identities. This being the case, attempting to be rigid and visibly intolerant of another culture will get you nowhere.

What is accepted by a particular group of people might be frowned upon by others. Consider this example: There are two settings—one is an American setting and the other is a Nigerian one. When talking to an individual in the American culture, it is usually expected that eye contact be made. Attempts to do otherwise can sometimes communicate that one is being dishonest or maybe even disrespectful. Most people in the Western environment live by this unwritten rule, kids and adults alike.

Alternatively, in some parts in Nigeria and most places on the African and Asian continents, the reverse is the case. Extended eye contact can be taken as being disrespectful or a challenge to authority. Occasional eye contact during the conversation is seen as more acceptable. Maintained eye contact is usually more acceptable if you are considered to be at the same level—perhaps the same age grade, peer group, and so on.

I brought up these examples to show how one thing can be acceptable to a group of people and unacceptable to others, so seeking to understand as opposed to demonizing is imperative. It is, therefore, pertinent that we appreciate these diversities and celebrate them.

If we don't seek to understand or care to adjust, we will create environments that increase the likelihood of miscommunication. We will resort to assuming instead of seeking answers about what we do not know. We need to fight against our regular instincts to only surround ourselves with cultures we are comfortable with and to prepare our subconscious to take in habits and reactions that are able to adjust to variances in the cultures around us. Now let's look into the four stages of cultural awareness. Please be honest with yourself as to which of these accurately describe you.

The Four Stages of Cultural Awareness

Understanding the stages of cultural awareness is important for both individuals and institutions. This understanding allows individuals and team members to communicate better as well as to collaborate toward a shared goal. The four stages are the Parochial stage, the Ethnocentric stage, the Synergistic stage, and the Participatory culture stage.

The Parochial Stage ("I only know my way")

Individuals in this stage are completely unaware of another way of life. They believe that their way is the only way. This stage can also be called blissful ignorance, because the concept of diversity or any other way of seeing things is foreign.

The Ethnocentric Stage ("I know their way, but mine is better")

Those who belong here are aware of other cultures but believe their way is better. They are usually enthusiastic about their cultures and brag about how they are the best to the point that they are critics of those from other identities, usually passing cynical moments and making jest of them. The pride they feel about their culture is usually at the expense of others.

The Synergistic Stage ("There are benefits to my way and other ways")

Individuals in this stage of cultural awareness recognize that there are cultural differences. They believe these differences can be beneficial and can contribute equally when collaborating to solve problems. They are aware of their own way of doing things as well as the ways of others. They choose the best approach depending on the situation they are faced with.

The Participatory Third Culture Stage ("You and I can create a new culture together")

This stage is characterized by an individual's ability to work with people of different cultures to create a culture of shared meanings. They can work with others to create new rules and cultures to meet the demands of any situation they find themselves in. When working with others, they both come up with a "third" culture.

∎ ∎ ∎

Which stage do you and your institution fall in? The objective of being culturally aware is to effectively maximize the diverse ideas and cultures that exist around you as well as gain appreciation for multiple ways to view solutions. This enables collaboration and communication to go smoothly. It also helps to avoid assumptions that lead to premature judgment, which leads to conflict.

The higher the degree of your cultural awareness the more understanding you will have of the values and behaviors of people from different backgrounds. Your cultural awareness is applicable to business settings, school environments, and daily interactions. It allows you to assess, analyze, interpret, and evaluate things from multiple perspectives. It provides you with the sensitivity needed for good communication to exist among groups that see the world differently. It limits generalizations and stereotypes.

26

How Parents Can Help Their Children Be Culturally Aware

Raising children in today's multicultural world can be incredibly confusing, but I want to encourage parents to foster more curiosity and open-mindedness. This section covers ways parents can do just this. Don't just teach these concepts to your children. Practice them. Remember, your kids are watching you. Practice what you preach.

Encourage Regular Interaction with Other Cultures

This sounds simple enough but is not always done. I always encourage parents to start this as early as possible so as to develop the habit of not seeing difference as "less than." Make efforts to go to places that usually have a good mix of people from different backgrounds, such as museums, festivals, events, and camps. When you take children to these kinds of locations, go a step further by also interacting with people there and asking people of other background open-ended questions about their cultures and languages. This communicates to children that you are okay with them meeting people from different backgrounds, a behavior they most likely will adopt.

I also encourage open dialogue here. Check in with children and engage in dialogue in order to hear their thoughts on what they have been exposed to.

Encourage Reading Diverse Books

The idea here is to read far and wide. When getting books for your kids, ensure that the authors are from multiple cultures. Authors usually write books based on their cultural frame of references and/or experiences so that means that your kids will be exposed to multiple cultural identities and backgrounds by reading. Their minds will be enlightened and more open to individuals from various parts of the world.

Encourage Respect and an Appreciation for Different-Sounding Names

I cannot count the amount of times people called me by my last name instead of my full first name, Akintayo, when I was younger, because they kept telling me that it was too weird-sounding. Even as I started to go by the shortened version of my first name, Tayo, people would tell me that my name should be spelled *Taio* since it is pronounced like *Tie-Yo*. The nerve! I always respond with "so because you don't want to make the effort to get my name right, I should change the spelling of my name to a Westernized format and erase my Nigerian identity?" to which they respond with, "uh … uh … not what I meant. I'm sorry."

It is normal for us to be familiar with the names of those from our tribes, region, and nation, but when we train our kids to put in an effort to pronounce what are to them difficult-sounding names, we teach them how to be more appreciative of other cultures. I can definitely tell you that it is not fun being laughed at because of your name. Something as simple as a name is a big part of one's identity, so let's train our kids to appreciate all names.

Use Food as a Way to Understand Other Cultures

Food is something all cultures enjoy, so encouraging your children to try different types of food while learning about the origins and significance of the meals is a way to enjoy while learning. Just like music and artwork, foods tell a lot about a set of individuals: what they believe in and how they interact with each other.

Encourage Critical Thinking as Opposed to Assumption

Developing critical thinking with kids at an early age allows for them to seek to understand first. Most of the world's problems of racism, tribalism, and cultural discrimination stem from a lack of willingness to understand. People are people; the fact that others aren't like us doesn't make them less than us, nor does that make us any more superior. All individuals, including you, were born into a particular society, culture, language, and geographical location. None of us chose any of these; it's just fate. So, encourage the habit of understanding instead of judging.

Encourage Language Learning

Acquiring new language skills is one of the best ways to improve cultural competency because as you learn a new language, you learn about the customs as well.

27

How Schools and Teachers Can Help Children Be Culturally Aware

O ther than parents, the greatest influences in a child's life during their formative years are their teachers. Teachers play a critical role in developing youth in many other ways. Sometimes teachers end up spending more time with children than the parents, so here are some ways teachers can teach children cultural awareness.

Appreciate and Celebrate the Cultural Backgrounds of Your Students

Always promote an inclusive environment that appreciates the full identity of your students. You can start with their names and their pronunciations and meaning. While each student shares facts about their cultures and customs, provide opportunities for them to educate the rest of the class on "why they do things the way they do."

After your students speak, take some time to analyze and celebrate the diversities in social behaviors, beliefs, norms, rites, music, and so on. Everyone has a culture, regardless of where they come from, so showcase the range. You must also be careful not to lean in the direction of a particular student or ethnicity.

Be Your Students' Leader and Not Their Dictator

There's a difference between these two. As someone who has lived in a dictatorship, I can tell you that there is barely any freedom of expression there. In your classroom, be clear about who the leader is but encourage open dialogue. Open up the floor for more interaction and engagement and avoid making it transactional.

Create a Curriculum That Respects and Includes All the People It Serves

A school curriculum should be a live document that is culturally responsive and reflective of the student body it serves. It is one that engages every student irrespective of color, race, language, or background. It can only be this inclusive if it acknowledges the differences that each student possesses and the fact that different students might need different things to be successful, thereby enhancing the inclusion of everyone.

Our academic institutions must realize that they have a duty to teach their students to understand that every other person is different from them, which doesn't make them inferior or superior. Our educational systems and the teachers must see their role as being pivotal in establishing culturally responsive students and society as a whole.

The Art of Our Lives

As I sat there watching her paint her portraits
and landscapes on the streets of New York City,
I pondered on how we approach the art of our
lives today.
In our fast-paced world of reactiveness and
radioactivity, we sometimes forget to paint our
full pictures.
I say this because most of us only see what's in
front of us and not what's around us.

We look at details without the context and so
we miss out on the aerial view of our
circumstances.

We ignore our subconscious and let our
conscious minds define our whole selves.
We look for others to complete us instead of
committing to filling ourselves up.
We use limited stories of people we don't know
to define "them."
We let moments of weaknesses become
people's defining characteristics.
We let our faults dampen our blessings.

But what if we found our inner artists and
decided to paint fuller pictures?
What if we ...
sketched out the problems in our lives before
going to the absolute?
painted the background before focusing on the
subjects?
used the brushes of our minds to add texture to
the sketches our biases have previously formed?

What if we focused on painting the full picture?

I think our canvases would look a lot different.
We'd see all the color that exists in our lives
and not just the black and white.

—Tayo Rockson

28

Applying LORA to Instead, Communicate

Remember that **LORA** is my acronym for Listen, Observe, Reflect, and Act, the system I developed as a way to apply every concept I explain; what's shown here is for the Instead, Communicate framework. As in earlier chapters, it's both a summary and an action plan, so take out your journals and make note of all these.

Listen

When you communicate, remember to keep in mind how you listen when you educate and how you listen when you are committing to fight against perpetuation. Remember to be an active listener by listening to learn, evaluate, and understand, and listen to the systems around you. Keep all this in mind as you listen to the facts instead of your opinion. Listen for common values to share.

Observe

- ◆ Observe moments you find yourself getting defensive, passive-aggressive, and aggressive in communication.
- ◆ Observe moments in your communication when your intention does not match the impact and moments when your intention matches impact.

Reflect

- Reflect on moments in the past when you practiced dehumanization in conflict. Why did you do so?
- Reflect on moments you ignored the issue of a conflict and attacked the person. Why did you do so?
- Do you make it an effort to understand the other person's motives and interests?
- Do you put down others while trying to make your point?
- Are you a willing teacher when someone makes a mistake around you? Reflect on whether you create paths to forgive or you are quick to cancel people if they offend you.

Act

- Watch YouTube channels like Jubilee, Cut, Skin Deep, and SoulPancake to gain insight into different perspectives, opposing views, and a whole spectrum of human emotions.
- Don't make being right the goal of your conversations.
- Commit to looking for the root cause in an argument instead of for someone to blame.
- Focus on behaviors people exhibit as opposed to personalities when addressing conflict.
- Commit to naming your emotions regularly and feeling them fully so you don't suppress them.
- Commit to keeping your conversations goal oriented.
- Avoid assumptions by legitimizing and echoing people's feelings back to them.
- Don't be afraid to admit when you are wrong or when you could have done better.
- Regularly communicate the takeaways in your conversations and apply learnings for next time.
- Commit to regularly creating space for open conversation and having open channels to address conflict.
- Know when to walk away from an argument.

The art of communication is the language of leadership. George Bernard Shaw once said, "The single biggest problem in communication is the illusion that it has taken place." And I couldn't agree more.

29

Use Your Difference to Make a Difference

I wrote this book to shine a light on the harmful social norms we have accepted, ignored, and perpetuated. Social norms we have made turned into cultures that cause exclusion. I wanted to shine a light on how today's social environments as presently constructed can lead to more harm and division. My hope is that as we become aware of these behaviors, our roles in the perpetuation of these behaviors, and make sense of our past, we get back to caring for each other and being more empathetic. After all, it is what most of us are wired to do. It's human nature.

Don't believe me? Virtually all of us (some more than others) have mirror neurons, or imitation biases, as they are sometimes called, that fire when our brain cells are activated, such as when you see someone smile and you find yourself immediately smiling back in response or when you see someone stub their toes and you immediately wince as if it had happened to you. The same thing happens when we see others yawn. Mirror neurons show that our brains are actually wired for empathy. According to Giacomo Rizzolatti, one of the neuroscientists who discovered these neurons, "We are social beings. Our survival depends on our understanding the actions, intentions, and emotions of others. Mirror neurons allow us to understand other people's mind, not only through conceptual reasoning but through imitation. Feeling, not thinking."[1]

We suffer greatly when our social bonds are threatened or severed. One aspect of human nature is to protect ourselves from harm. I find that, in the name of self-preservation, we have defined the wrong things as threats. I hope that as you have gone through this book, you have begun to see how a lot these so-called threats fuel our biases and promote misinformation and that negative systems have created false narratives of division. The things that cause division, like patriarchy, slavery, and homophobia are all human creations. We need to challenge ourselves to do better. As a generation, let us be greater than our worst impulses and create more inclusive environments and celebrate intersectional identities. It is harder to turn to hatred when we understand the lived experiences of others.

Valuing Collaboration

We need to develop our cultural intelligence and recognize that not everyone sees the world through the same cultural frame of reference that we do. We need to understand our own cultural assumptions and stereotypes and how they influence others and their behaviors. This takes understanding the value of the people you lead and the people around you. The best way to do this is to include them in every conversation you're having. The key to inclusion is engagement, and that means actively seeking input. Great connectors recognize this and so they prioritize collaboration.

What we all can do as connectors is to create a personal board of directors that includes people from different backgrounds. By purposefully spending time with people with very different worldviews from you, you develop the ability to see things from a macro and micro level. If you're an executive, that means you are intentionally surrounding yourself with people who think differently from you. If you're an entrepreneur, you're in constant conversations with mentors who bring different perspectives. If you're an online personality, you're creating groups with the social platforms you're involved in and engaging with people from different backgrounds in conversations around your industry.

You want to make sure that the people who feel the most different understand that they belong. You want to want to make sure that the quietest in the group understands they have a voice, and this starts with you inviting them to the table. Inclusion requires us to actively commit to being open to learning and embracing new ways of thinking, doing, and behaving. Start to do this and watch as the walls we have created collapse and become bridges—bridges to connection.

Connecting via Technology

As far as technology goes, great connectors understand how to use this equalizer to connect humans. They use technology to educate and provide opportunities for everyone on the table. At any time, you can connect with whoever you want whenever you want. When you put down this book, many of you will immediately look at your phone. Heck, some of you might have been doing it right now as you are reading and you are connecting with people who are not physically here. Research shows that this trend is only going to continue. Gartner estimates that by 2020, there will be about 20 billion Internet-connected things in the world.[2] That includes more than just computers and mobile devices.

Whether you like it or not, we are in a very, very connected world.

We're sharing with each other, human to human, in a very real way. We're no longer limited by the geography of where we live and who we know. Inclusive leaders recognize this and start to use this fact to create supportive, interactive communities based on common interests.

Instead of pushing people apart or turning them into machines, inclusive leaders understand how to use technology to make us become more human and connect with each other as we never could before.

Sandy Hoffman, a diversity and inclusion executive, said, "It's critical that the human connection is aligned with the technology connection to allow the power of collaboration through Inclusion."

Inclusion Beats Division *Every* Time!

Leaders of tomorrow must know how to succeed with all these differences. We must attempt to understand our changing world so that we can leverage our differences the right way. My concern with the world today is that too many people are not listening to each other. In fact, many people have responded to the changes that I mentioned earlier with fear and anger instead of love and understanding. But I believe that there's hope, and I believe that we can change the world. It is no easy task, but there are two reasons why people don't believe they can change the world today: fixed mindsets and limited worldviews.

We can't afford to be shortsighted, because when you change the way you see things, the things you see change. Individuals with a fixed mindset seek to validate themselves. Individuals with a growth mindset focus on developing themselves.

The work to change the world does not end at the offices of law enforcement or governments. It begins with us, in our backyards, our families, our schools, our spheres of influence, and our minds.

All of us are leaders in some shape or form and we are growing up among each other, so our actions matter. We are each a symbol in some way. We can be symbols of love and hope or symbols of hate and intolerance.

There's a lack of trust in our world because most people refuse to accept responsibility for their actions or acknowledge the power that comes with their privileges.

So I want you all to be aware of the actions you take, because what we all decide to do in public and private has the potential to influence policies today and tomorrow. Let's make sure those actions are improving our self-awarenesses, acknowledging our biases, celebrating the differences around us, finding common ground, and being a voice for the voiceless. Let's practice courage.

To this point, I remember watching one of my favorite comedians, Hasan Minhaj, say something in his Netflix stand-up special *Homecoming King* that really struck me. He was recounting a story in which his father told him something he would never forget. His father said: "Your courage to do what's right has to be greater than your fear of getting hurt. So Hasan be brave, Hasan be brave."[3]

Powerful. So I want to challenge you to brave. Choose to do what is right over what hurts.

History is made by those who have the courage to act, and so my call to action for you all today is to educate and make sure you don't perpetuate. Instead, communicate. The fact of the matter is that you have a choice. You can choose to see a world and do nothing about it or you can choose to see a world that is hurting and participate in changing the narrative.

Whichever choice you make, you are changing the world in some way. My hope is that you choose to do the latter. And so I end with this question.

Will you use your difference to make a difference?

Notes

1. Andrea García Cérdan, "Mirror Neurons: The Most Powerful Tool," *CogniFit* (blog), 8 June 2017, blog.cognifit.com/mirror-neurons/.

2. https://www.gartner.com/imagesrv/books/iot/iotEbook_digital.pdf.

3. "Hasan Minhaj: Homecoming King," Netflix, 23 May 2017, www.netflix.com/title/80134781.

Educate, Don't Perpetuate. Instead, Communicate.

Glossary

Affinity bias: A bias that occurs when we see someone we feel we have an affinity with (e.g., we support the same teams, we attended the same college, we come from the same place, or they remind us of someone we know and like).

Allies: People from dominant groups who actively work to tear down oppression.

Apartheid: A world where you, your spouse, and your kid cannot connect because of the color of your skin.

Attribution bias: How we explain behavior or the cause and effect of something. It's attaching meaning to something, so attribution bias would be attributing someone's behavior to their intrinsic nature.

Beauty bias: How we judge people based on their physical appearance, especially when they are considered attractive.

Bias journal: A journal in which you document biases you have as well as track how you will unpack them.

Cancel culture: A term used to refer to the phenomenon of "canceling," or no longer morally, financially, and/or digitally supporting people—usually celebrities—or things that many have deemed unacceptable or problematic.

Colonialism: Telling people that, based on their language, tribe, or religion, they were unable to connect.

Colonization: The act or process of settling among and establishing control over the indigenous people of an area. It involves appropriating a place or environment for one's own use.

Confirmation bias: The tendency to gather and process information by looking for, or interpreting, information that is consistent with your existing beliefs.

Conformity bias: The tendency to behave like those around you rather than using your own personal judgment, even if it's against your personal interest.

Connection: The ability to connect with self, purpose, others, and the world.

Contrast effect or contrast bias: The tendency to enhance or diminish something in a large grouping after a single comparison with one of its peers; it doesn't factor in the whole group.

Crusades: A series of religious wars fought because of an unwillingness to connect with foreign religions.

Cultural awareness: The recognition of our cultural traits, such as language, beliefs, art, music, values, history, and perception.

Disinformation: The dissemination of false information, rumors, hoaxes, or propaganda with the intent to mislead and influence public opinion.

Echo chamber: An environment in which a person encounters only beliefs or opinions that coincide with their own, so that their existing views are reinforced and alternative ideas are not considered.

Employer brand: The process of articulating your company's unique message, voice, and strategy, and attracting the right candidates to your company.

Enslavement: The act of making someone a slave. This usually involves forced migration, suppression, and oppression.

Equality: Treating everyone the same way.

Equity: Giving everyone what they need to be successful.

Ethnocentrism: Judging other cultures based solely on the values and standards of one's own culture.

Finding Your Inner Sherlock: This refers to one's ability to deduce and observe what is going on around you effectively.

Gender bias: A preference or prejudice toward one gender over the other.

Genocide: The urge to wipe out a part of an ethnic, racial, religious, or national group because of a refusal to connect.

Halo effect: One characteristic of a person causing you to view that person positively.

Hidden immigrant: Someone who is able to look and sound pretty much like everyone else in their "home" country but, due to a TCK upbringing or other extensive overseas living, is not quite as native as the natives.

Horns effect: The direct opposite of the halo effect and it occurs when a characteristic about a person negatively impacts how you view him or her.

Identity: Largely concerned with the two questions "Who am I?" and "What does it mean to be who I am?," identity relates to our basic values that dictate the choices we make (e.g., relationships, school, career).

Imperialism: A state government, practice, or advocacy of extending power and dominion, especially by direct territorial acquisition or by gaining political and economic control of other areas.

Intersectionality: The theory that the overlap of various social identities, such as race, gender, sexuality, and class, contributes to the specific type of systemic oppression and discrimination experienced by an individual.

LORA: Acronym for the Listen, Observe, Reflect, and Act model used to apply concepts in frameworks.

Microaggressions: A term that has been used in academic circles since the 1970s to describe small casual verbal and behavioral indignities against people of color, women, people with disabilities, immigrants, young or old people, and so forth. They are regular verbal, nonverbal, and environmental slights, snubs, or insults that can be intentional or unintentional.

Nationalism I mean Populism I mean Isolationism: A refusal to connect with other nations except on your own terms.

Negativity bias: Focusing on the negative aspects of what is happening around us.

Oppression: Forces that use power dynamics to limit opportunities and growth for people of different groups by systematically taking away their identities and power.

Oppression Olympics: A term used when two or more groups compete or engage in conversations to prove that their marginalized group is more oppressed than the other.

Othering: Viewing and/or treating a person or group of people as different from oneself in such a way that you alienate them. This can result in hostility and dehumanization toward people of different race, ethnicity, religion, culture, gender, country, sexual orientation, etc.

Personhood: The status or condition of being a person.

Pop culture: The mix of ideas, videos, images, attitudes, and perspectives that characterize a given culture and is loved and accepted by the mainstream population.

Positivity bias: People evaluating an individual positively even when they have negative evaluations of the group to which that individual belongs.

Power dynamics: The way different people or different groups of people interact with each other and where one of these sides is more powerful than the other one.

Privilege: A special right, advantage, or immunity granted or available only to a particular person or group of people.

Propaganda: Biased or misleading pieces of information used to promote or publicize a particular political cause or point of view.

Racism: A refusal to connect with someone who has a different skin color.

Recruiters: Individuals who work to fill job openings in businesses or organizations. Their job requirements typically include reviewing candidate's job experiences, negotiating salaries, and placing candidates in agreeable employment positions.

Segregation: Telling people that they couldn't connect because they looked different.

Slavery: Telling people that they were subhuman so couldn't possibly connect.

Sourcing: The act of finding a candidate profile you want to follow up on.

Sphere of influence: Anyone in your circle who has the power to influence you or you have the ability to influence—your friends, family, significant others, teachers, or mentors.

Talent acquisition team: The team that is responsible for finding, acquiring, assessing, and hiring candidates to fill the roles that are required to meet company goals and fill project requirements. Talent acquisition professionals are usually skilled not only in sourcing tactics, candidate assessment, and compliance and hiring standards, but also in employment branding practices and corporate hiring initiatives.

Third-culture kid, or TCK: Someone who spent the formative periods of their lives outside of their parents' cultures.

Troll farm: An organized operation of many users who may work together in a "factory" or from different places across a distributed network to generate online traffic aimed at affecting public opinion and to spread misinformation and disinformation.

About the Author

Tayo (pronounced TIE-OH) Rockson is a speaker, consultant, brand strategist, and media personality who runs UYD Management—a strategic leadership and consulting firm that helps organizations incorporate sustainable diversity and inclusion practices. As someone who has lived on four continents, Tayo is an authority on communicating effectively across cultures and describes himself as a cultural translator. He hosts the very popular podcast *As Told By Nomads*, which features interviews with global nomads, third-culture kids, and entrepreneurs discussing what it takes to be global leaders.

He has spoken at TEDx multiple times, as well as at the World Bank and the United Nations Foundation, among many other places, and his work has been seen on *NowThis News*, *BuzzFeed*, *Forbes*, *Huffington Post*, *Entrepreneur, Inc.*, and *Global Living Magazine*. He was recently named a top millennial influencer to watch in 2018 by *New Theory Mag* and his "Art of Diplomacy" TED talk was named one of the 11 TED talks that will make you a better entrepreneur by 99designs, along with the likes of Simon Sinek, Mel Robbins, and the late John Wooden.

Tayo regularly works on projects involving leadership, branding, and cross-cultural communication. In his spare time, he loves staying active by playing basketball, soccer, and tennis. He is probably the biggest LeBron James fan out there.

Index

Page references followed by *fig* indicate an illustrated figure.